The "What's for Dinner?" Solution

Kathi Lipp

HARVEST HOUSE PUBLISHERS

EUGENE, OREGON

Cover design by Left Coast Design, Portland, Oregon

Cover illustration © Krieg Barrie

Published in association with the literary agency of WordServe Literary Group, Ltd., 10152 S. Knoll Circle, Highlands Ranch, CO 80130

THE "WHAT'S FOR DINNER?" SOLUTION
Copyright © 2011 by Kathi Lipp
Published by Harvest House Publishers
Eugene, Oregon 97402
www.harvesthousepublishers.com

Library of Congress Cataloging-in-Publication Data
    Lipp, Kathi, 1967-
    The what's for dinner solution / Kathi Lipp.
        p. cm.
    ISBN 978-0-7369-3837-2 (pbk.)
    ISBN 978-0-7369-4209-6 (eBook)
    1. Dinners and dining. 2. Quick and easy cooking. 3. Cookbooks. I. Title.
    TX737.L57 2011
    641.5—dc22

                                                    2011008138

Printed in the United States of America

        11 12 13 14 15 16 17 18 19 / LB-SK / 10 9 8 7 6 5 4 3 2 1

To my four favorite food testers:
Amanda, Jeremy, Justen, and Kimber.

Roger and I consider it among our hugest blessings
that the four of you will still come home for dinner.

Acknowledgments

LaRae Weikert, as well as Brad and Arlene Moses, for brainstorming with me and Roger and being the encouragers (and instigators) that you are.

Mom—for teaching me there was more to cooking than baking, and for feeding me and my kids when my life was at its hardest. Coming home to dinner made many things OK during a pretty rough time.

The Lipps—who love us and feed us when we travel.

Betty Dobson—who's given Roger his food culture of noodles and mashed potatoes (the one point in our marriage where we will never agree).

Brian, Lucinda, and Elsa—who love food as much as we do and share their love (and goodies) with us.

To every woman who contributed her wisdom and recipes to this book, especially Ruth Shave, Regena Florenti, Vashie Miller, Ann Stea, Linda Carlblom, Martha Orlando, Robin Dilallo, Amy Redelsperger, and Linda Jenkins.

Some of my favorite six chicks (and a dude)—Tonya Walters, Vikki Francis, Shari Wideman, Penny and Elliot Sands, Kelli Simmerok, Lynette Furstenberg, and Melanie Bernard.

My amazing team—Sunnie Weber, Monica Trevino, Ginny Chapman, Angela Bowen, Kimberly Hunter, and Linda Jenkins.

My editor, Rod Morris, whose infinite patience was constantly tested during this editing, and who still makes the process fun.

Rachelle Gardner, my super-agent, who kept telling me (almost always at dinnertime), "Would you hurry up and finish the book? I *need* it."

Erin MacPherson—my foodie friend and a constant encouragement.

Lonette Whitaker and Debbie McDonald, who have invested time, wisdom, and countless lunches in me. I'm proud to call you friends.

Roger—my favorite BBQer, hole-in-the-wall finder, salsa and guac maker. You like food spicy; I like it when my food doesn't hurt. With food and with life, you challenge me to try new things, be adventurous, and kick it up a notch. Love you, baby.

Contents

Why *The "What's for Dinner?" Solution?*

Are you traumatized by dinner?

Oh, I know. You know that dinner is supposed to happen every single night. You know that around six o'clock, hungry mouths are going to turn to you to feed them. Everyone is looking to you and asking the same question: "What's for dinner?"

And they are expecting you to have an answer.

But that's not when the panic sets in. No, you've been thinking about dinner for a while. There was a brief nod to it this morning as you were running out the door to work, but no time to really do anything about it. OK, that eliminates anything that required defrosting.

And at lunch, you thought, *Maybe I should look up some recipes online for something for tonight.* But you can't remember what ingredients you have at home (and more importantly, what condition they're in), so you go to plan C—drop by the supermarket on the way home.

So there you are at 5:15 at the grocery store with no doable plan, just a hope and a prayer for some inspiration as the prospect of yet another rotisserie chicken looms large.

Or maybe you're a stay-at-home mom who thinks, *I have all day to get dinner on the table, but why does it have to take me all day to do it?* (Perhaps it's the two toddlers hanging off your legs? But I digress...)

I want you to stop the madness.

Like me, you may love to cook, but the problem with dinner is that it comes every single night. Doesn't matter whether I feel like cooking or not. Doesn't matter whether I've found a great new recipe that inspires me. Doesn't matter if anyone will actually eat it or not.

I love cooking. I really do. But sometimes I just don't love to cook. Dinner is just so…well, daily.

If I don't go into my week with a plan for dinner (it's a lot easier to wing it for breakfast and lunch around our house), we usually end up eating a lot of takeout and fast food with a huge side of guilt.

But when I go in with a plan, that all changes:

- I don't spend my day worrying about what we're going to have for dinner, because I already know what we're having.

- I don't spend my lunch hour looking for recipes that require little more than baking soda and batteries (the two things in my fridge I know haven't expired).

- I don't feel guilty about running past my freezer with all the meat in there waiting to be defrosted.

- I don't spend money on non-nutritional dinners from places where I have to order through an intercom.

So how does this all work? Glad you asked. Here's the plan. By the time you finish this book, I want you to:

- Plan your meals for a month, and then eat (most of) them at home.

- Get out of your cooking ruts and put all your tools to work.

- Have a kitchen that works for you.

- Have some fun along the way.

Six Quick Steps to Get Started with
The "What's For Dinner?" Solution
(I promise—they really *are* easy!)

1. Read through the entire book.

This is your chance to get a feel for the master plan. Go ahead and make notes in the margins, change up some ingredients in the recipes, whatever!

2. Find two friends (at least) to plan with you.

It doesn't matter if they're phone friends, Internet buddies, or face-to-face girlfriends you meet with at Starbucks down the street. Location is not important; company is. Figure out a time to spend together (after everyone has read through the book) to come up with a plan for when and how you're going to plan your meals and make it happen—maybe a joint cooking day or a freezer-meal swap? These friends will be the ones who share their favorite recipes with you, while you let them know when frozen chicken breasts go on sale.

If you're doing this as a group, be sure to check out all the free group resources on our website: www.ProjectsForYourSoul.com. There are lots of helpful tools, forms, and other fun stuff to make this a great group project.

3. Decide on a start date.

Your start date can be tomorrow or two weeks from now. Mark it in a big bold way on your kitchen calendar. Set up reminders on your computer. I definitely recommend that you give yourself a couple of days to get ramped up and pull together a plan that you're excited about.

4. Come up with your plan.

You decide what steps you're going to take each day. I've provided a variety of ideas, but it's up to you to decide how you'll carry it out.

5. Share your plan with your friends.

I recommend that you make copies of your calendar to share with your friends. Not only does that give you accountability in making sure you get dinner on the table, but each of you will be inspired by the others. There is a Meal Planning Calendar at www.ProjectsForYourSoul .com you can download and print.

6. Be flexible.

If one of the meals you've planned for a certain day doesn't line up with your life that day, swap it for one that will work. The intention of *The "What's For Dinner?" Solution* is not to add stress, but to feed your family with less stress and more joy.

Part One

Get Prepared

Chapter 1

Girl Meets Kitchen, or Not Necessarily a Love Story

*"Happy and successful cooking doesn't rely only on know-how;
it comes from the heart, makes great demands on the palate and
needs enthusiasm and a deep love of food to bring it to life."*

GEORGES BLANC, FROM *MA CUISINE DES SAISONS*

I was not the kind of kid who grew up at my mom's knee, helping her chop carrots for Sunday night's chicken soup. I never really helped with any meal preparation, preferring to turn my attention in the kitchen to baking. There was always some social event with friends or a youth group party where I needed to bring brownies. The one memorable time I tried to make instant potatoes? Instead of the specified one-quarter tablespoon of salt, I used a quarter cup salt. That incident happened over twenty-five years ago, and I have yet to stop hearing about it from my loving and encouraging family.

Suffice to say, I was a bit ill-prepared for the cooking adventures that lay ahead as I lived on my own for the first time. And to complicate matters? My first apartment was in Uji, Japan, approximately seven thousand miles from my mother's loving embrace and her pot-roast recipe (as if I could afford beef in Japan).

The recipe cards were stacked against me. No cooking skills to speak of, living in a foreign land where most of the time I couldn't identify what I was eating much less figure out how it was prepared, a kitchen the size of my coat closet back home, and an oven so small it made me long for the Easy-Bake one of my childhood.

I was terrified going to the supermarket without an escort and a translator. I didn't speak the language (as a short-term missionary teaching conversational English, speaking Japanese was actually a disadvantage in my job), and as unfamiliar as I was with food shopping in the U.S., shopping in Uji was like watching a foreign movie without subtitles and then having to write a paper on the plot.

Oh, and eating out? So not an option. While my cooking skills were limited, my food budget was near nonexistent.

A few things were easy to recognize. The bread in Japan was amazing. It was buttery and flaky and perfect. And there was some really lovely cheese and ham. So, for the first three months of exploring this exotic new culture, I ate ham and cheese sandwiches *every single night* for dinner.

As I started to get to know some of my students and coworkers better, I had this urge to invite them over to hang out with me. But I had a sneaking suspicion they would want to be fed. I knew that my students would love some authentic American dishes. The question was, Who would I get to cook them?

Another short-term missionary, Diana, had a cookbook called *More-With-Less*. This wonderful little book produced by the Mennonite community had tons of recipes that used simple ingredients most cooks would have in their kitchen. While I didn't have a lot of pantry staples in my four-story walk-up, I was now armed with a grocery list as well as an English-to-Japanese dictionary for my trips to the store.

I started to look for simple things I could make: salads, sandwiches, curries, and mini-pizzas out of English muffins and ketchup. (I promise, my culinary skills *and* taste have gotten better over the years.) As I grew braver in all things cuisine, I started to ask my mom to send some of my favorite recipes from back home.

In fact, when I threw a Christmas celebration with my friend Spenser in my micro-sized apartment, we managed to make a fondue-potless version of my mom's Pizza Fondue. Shopping for the ingredients proved challenging, even for Spenser who spoke near-fluent Japanese. After several attempts to translate *cornstarch* into the native language (One would think corn + starch = cornstarch, right? Wrong. It's pronounced *korunstarcha*.), we headed back to my kitchen and made one of the best meals I have ever eaten—lots of tomato sauce, some ground beef, loads of cheese, and just the right amount of *korunstarcha.*

• • • • • • • • • • **Pizza Fondue** • • • • • • • • • •
(Connie Richerson)

½ lb. ground beef

1 small onion, chopped

2 10½-oz. cans pizza sauce (I use marinara sauce)

1 T. cornstarch (or *korunstarcha*, if you prefer)

1½ tsp. oregano

¼ tsp. garlic powder

2 cups cheddar cheese, shredded

1 cup mozzarella cheese, shredded

1 loaf French bread

Brown the ground beef and onion; drain. Put meat, sauce, cornstarch, and spices in fondue pot. When cooked and bubbly, add cheese. Spear crusty French bread cubes, then dip and swirl in fondue. This is also delicious with breadsticks. Serves 4 to 6.

• •

From that point on, I was hooked on collecting my favorite recipes. I bought my own copy of *More-With-Less* when I got back to the States, and when I got married a few months later, I received my very first copy of everyone's favorite red-and-white-plaid *Better Homes and Gardens New Cook Book,* with every recipe an emerging home cook could want.

I think most of us home cooks have a similar story to tell. OK, you probably didn't have your first significant cooking experience in Uji, Japan, but I bet the first few times you got dinner on the table all on your own, you might as well have been in a different country.

Maybe your mom had you peeling potatoes before you could walk. Maybe you have a rich heritage of recipes passed down from your grandmother. None of our cooking histories are going to look the same, but we do have one thing in common: We all need to get dinner on the table.

I am not a professional cook. Tom Colicchio will never be critiquing my braised kale and chocolate with bacon foam on *Top Chef*. But over the past twenty years I have put dinner on the table almost every single night. And while my family still likes a pizza from the neighborhood shop, our kids who have left home really look forward to coming back for a home-cooked meal.

That is all the reward I need.

Why This Book?

So, you discovered my deep dark secret—I'm not a professional chef. I don't have my own show on Food Network, my own brand of spatulas, and I'm not going to be appearing on any morning show making a frittata for Kathie Lee Gifford.

Still, I'm required to feed our large family almost daily. So when I come across a cookbook, I have an unnatural need to own it. I'm always looking for new recipes to keep dinner interesting at our house. I have an entire bookshelf in my kitchen for my ever-growing collection.

But to be honest with you, most of the money I've spent on those cookbooks could have been better spent on a good set of knives or a heavy iron skillet.

I have found that most cookbooks are aimed at the fantasy life many of us aspire to—entertaining regularly, having unusual and exotic ingredients on hand, and hours and hours in the kitchen to create these masterpieces, from scratch.

And then there is my reality. Yes, sometimes I like to spend a Saturday afternoon cooking up a big feast for friends and family. But most days? I want to get a delicious, healthy meal on the table quickly.

My test when I'm purchasing new cookbooks? I flip to a half dozen or so recipes throughout the book and ask myself, *Can I imagine cooking this recipe in the next couple of weeks?* If most of the recipes fail the test, the book stays at the store.

I want the reality. I want dinner on the table every night without being seduced by pictures of stylist-arranged food that—let's be honest—I'm *never* going to prepare.

While those books offer up a lot of grilled-chicken-in-a-peanut-sauce-in-the-sky dreams, I need some reality. It's not just about the recipe; it's about all the aspects of getting dinner on the table.

By the end of this book, my hope for you is that you will be able to:

- save time, money, and energy when it comes to preparing meals
- have less stress when it comes to shopping
- get your kitchen prepared for battle
- learn some stress-free ways to get dinner on the table
- get out of your cooking rut

This book is all about the process, the *how* of getting dinner on the table. It reflects the collective wisdom of hundreds of women who don't have prep cooks or a crew of interns trying out new recipes. We are the women who spend a significant part of our days thinking about, shopping for, and preparing dinner. And all these wise, wonderful women are going to show you a better way to get dinner on the table no matter what your cooking background or skill level.

This is the book I wish I'd had when I first started cooking, as well as when I was raising my brood of pint-sized food critics.

Don't worry, there will be plenty of recipes. We all love to find that one recipe that is going to become a family favorite! But this book has much more than that. My hope is that you will be able to use the recipes you already have, the ones in this book, and the new ones you find along the way to set a big, bountiful table for your family.

Chapter 2

It's Not Just About the Food

*"One cannot think well, love well,
sleep well, if one has not dined well."*

VIRGINIA WOOLF

My friend Dana Jarzynka sent this to me when we were talking about how important food is to the men in our lives:

> Kathi, my kindergartner, Jack, had to complete the sentence, "If I were President…" Here's what he wrote: "1. I wood pik up grbich [garbage], 2. I wood help the Urth, 3. I wood like sumwn [someone] to cook for me."

If that doesn't clearly express the relationship between men and food, I don't know what does. Food is really, really important to most men.

My husband, Roger, is no caveman. He was a single dad and did more than his fair share of getting dinner on the table for thirteen years. So it was great when we first got married. He was just so grateful for every meal that I cooked (and that clean underwear showed up regularly in his drawer without him having to think about it—total bonus). For me, it was a revelation to be thanked every night for cooking. I basked in the glory…for a few months.

After a while, we settled into a routine of me cooking dinner and Roger saying a polite thank you after the table was cleared. (Let's be clear—I completely understand that a thank you is more than most women get for making dinner every night.) After a while, though, the meals degenerated more or less into, "Hey, if you want to eat something, perhaps you should fix it" standoffs. There was just a bit of bitterness and resentment at having to be the one who almost always made dinner happen.

Don't you just love that Christ-like servant attitude that poured out of me?

It took me a long while to realize that my new do-it-yourself approach wasn't benefiting *anyone* in our house.

Making Men Feel Loved Through Spaghetti

When I was working on my first book, *The Husband Project*, I set about doing a very unscientific research project: Find out what men like.

I know, I know. If you've been conscious for any amount of time in the twenty-first century, the answer is obvious. If you are married (and if your marriage were a house), the world tells you that the place your husband wants to spend his time is in the bedroom.

And that's true—to a point.

But guess what? There's more to that answer. With the guys I interviewed, the answer was twofold: the bedroom *and* the kitchen.

When it came to discovering ways to make men feel loved and cared for, food was way at the top of the list.

- They loved when their wives made their favorite chocolate cake for no reason.
- They loved when there was dinner in the oven after a long day of work.
- They loved when their wives would stop by the bakery to pick up their favorite éclair.
- They loved when their wives would leave little treats around the house of the candy persuasion.

I knew that food was important to my husband (he takes his steaks and his salsa *very* seriously), but what was amazing to see as my boys grew up was how important food became to them as well. While my daughter Kimber will ask "When is dinner?" so she can plan the rest of her very busy social life, my boys want to know "What's for dinner?"

We regularly have Every Man For Himself (EMFH) nights when I'm working out of town (and trust me, there are always enough fixin's in the fridge to put together something yummy), and each of the kids can cook for themselves. Buuuuutttttt when I'm around, all three of the men who live in this house love it when I cook.

I have come to find out that there's a special security for men when they are being fed. I love how my friend Mark put it, "My wife gets a sense of security from me bringing home a paycheck every other week. It's the same for me and dinner. When I come home and there's something cooking, somehow it just gives me a sense of security—like everything is right in the world."

Now please don't read me wrong. I'm not saying it's all up to the womenfolk of the house to get dinner on the table. My hubby not only knows what a spatula is, he knows how to use it. However, in most of the families I know, at least 51 percent of the meal planning, shopping, cooking, and cleaning up are the woman's responsibility. But hey, if you're a guy reading this book, you get major bonus points.

And understanding that getting food on the table is not just a food thing but an act of love can make feeding the troops a bit more rewarding.

Blended Family v. The Brady Bunch

In a blended family like ours, keeping this perspective was especially important. When Roger and I got married, he and his kids had been by themselves for a long time. I'll be honest, Jeremy, Roger's youngest, was none too thrilled that we were getting married. (Would you be after having your dad to yourself for almost thirteen years?)

I honestly thought that if I could just love Jeremy enough, we could be that episode of *The Brady Bunch* where Bobby worries about being a stepchild and Carol, the mom, says, "The only steps in this house are the ones that go upstairs."

Riiiiiiight.

For most of us, blending families feels like putting everyone in a blender. Those touching scenes and very-Brady moments are few and far between.

But there were a couple of ways I could show love to Jeremy without ever having to say it.

Laundry and lasagna.

As a single dad, Roger did a great job getting food on the table and keeping the Health Department at bay. But with working full-time, serving at church, and raising two kids, Roger's go-to dinner plan more often than not involved a debit card and a drive-through.

You would think that would be a kid's dream come true, and for a while, I'm sure both Jeremy and his sister, Amanda, loved the freedom of getting to choose the meals they wanted.

But Jeremy—like most men, no matter their age—loves food.

And Jeremy loved knowing that someone was cooking for him.

When I looked at my dinner prep through his eyes, it changed the way I approached getting food on the table. When I saw feeding him as an act of love, an act of service, it completely changed my attitude. I got excited about those lasagna dinners again. It became my secret mission: To show Jeremy that I loved and valued him, without telling him that I loved and valued him. (If you've ever been part of a blended family, or even just had a surly teenage boy in the house, you know exactly what I'm talking about.)

Dinner is about so much more than the food.

It's about connecting with the people we love.

It's about serving the people we love.

Dinner is the one time during the day when, after the food is on the table, we can sit across from the people we love and pour into each other's day.

So on the days that you are feeling resentful that it's time to feed all these people—again!—remember you have a gift to share. The gift of telling the people in your life:

- You are loved.
- You are cared for.
- Something routine is going on in your house.

I understand if you're feeling a bit of resentment about dinner. I'm sure you spend a big portion of your day figuring out what's for dinner and then cooking it without a whole lot of appreciation.

My hope is that by the end of this book, you'll get some fresh ideas about how to get dinner on the table. *But* my bigger hope is that you'll see getting dinner on the table as an act of love that you are performing every single day.

And hey, if no one else is noticing, let me just tell you: Good job!

Chapter 3

How to Save Time, Save Money, Save Your Sanity

"I feel a recipe is only a theme, which an intelligent cook can play each time with a variation."

MADAM BENOIT

When it comes to cooking, as with all things in life, your priorities are going to change.

When I was a young bride still trying to figure out how to feed my husband and me without necessitating trips to the hospital, we had the gift of time. I was working only part-time, so time wasn't an issue. But money was. I had no idea how to prepare meals, much less do so affordably.

In the next phase of our lives, finances were still a priority, but now new factors had reared their cute little heads—Justen and Kimberly. When I was caring just for Justen, things still seemed slightly manageable. He was one of those trick kids—he slept and cooed and snuggled and slept, lulling you into that false sense of security, "Hey, this isn't so hard. Maybe we could have another baby." And that is when God sends you the child who doesn't sleep, screams as if you're poking her with a cattle prod every time a stranger looks at her, and causes a whole group of nursery workers at church to take an early retirement. Welcome Kimberly.

Now, not only was money a factor, so was the hassle of cooking. I no longer had long afternoons to pore over cookbooks. With two kids under the age of two, my trips to the grocery store were a major expedition that I wanted to limit as much as possible. And since the only position that Kimberly found tolerable was in my arms, any recipe that required more than three steps seemed somehow insurmountable.

As the kids got older, I got a little better about getting dinner that was both edible and affordable on the table. But then I went back to work.

My first job after the kids were in school could not have been more convenient—I became the secretary at the tiny Christian school they were both attending. (The tiny Christian school with the not-so-tiny tuition is what necessitated the new job.) Suddenly, money was not the only issue. So was time.

And so it goes. Sometimes money is more precious than time. At other times, the kid-and-job-and-jam-packed-schedule craziness reminds you that you just need to keep things simple.

I have gone through all these phases. When I homeschooled. When we had no money. When I worked full-time. When we had no time. And even now, when I'm on a book deadline and all my brainpower is going into the words on the page and not so much the food in the fridge.

In the next few chapters, I want to share some of the things I've learned that can help you cope with whatever stage of life you are in. Whatever is stressing you out right now—saving time, saving money, or saving your sanity (or even all three)—I understand. You're just having a hard time getting dinner on the table and the pressure is coming from every side. Take a deep breath, read through these chapters, and see what would be easy for you to apply right away.

And let me give you a little hope if you are feeling overwhelmed. Just by reading this book and putting a few of these steps into action, you are already making progress toward saving time, money, and energy. Just having a vague, planned-on-the-back-of-an-envelope idea of what you are going to eat will make you feel calmer and more peaceful about the whole situation.

Save Time

Think Ahead

When you plan out your meals for the week (or month), you save all those back-and-forth trips to the grocery store to pick up the little items you need for each meal. Having a plan eliminates all that "What's for dinner?" stress and lets you go into your evening with peace instead of panic.

Even if, right this moment, you grabbed a paper napkin and scribbled down seven meals you want to have over the next week—without checking your fridge or what's on sale or what your kid's soccer schedule is, even without checking your calendar for the week or running to the grocery store—just having that list will start to lessen your stress and will save you time.

Here's my list for the next week:

> *Monday*—Grilled sausages with potatoes and veggies
>
> *Tuesday*—Vegetarian lasagna, bread-machine bread, salad
>
> *Wednesday*—Asian stir-fry with rice and a mandarin-orange salad
>
> *Thursday*—Chicken cacciatore and no-butter smashed potatoes
>
> *Friday*—Pita pizzas and Italian salad
>
> *Saturday*—Chicken chili and whole-wheat breadsticks
>
> *Sunday*—Slow-cooker apple pork roast with ratatouille

Immediately, your mind starts skipping ahead, *What if I'm not home in time to make the lasagna on Tuesday? Do I have pitas at home?*

Don't panic.

Just write the menu down. Let it sit for a second. Later, you can look at what's already in your fridge, what your schedule is this week, and adjust from there.

So many of us fail to plan because we're waiting for the perfect time to sit down and make a menu, look at our calendars, take an inventory of everything we have, look at what's on sale and so on. And those are all good things. But really—you're waiting for a lot of stars to align.

So make a bad meal plan and adjust it later. Oh the time you will save.

The Magic List

Every home has that magnetized list hanging on the fridge where every person over the age of twelve or so is supposed to write down any item that needs to be purchased at the grocery store. A few years ago, my son Justen was helping me unpack groceries and was irritated that I didn't purchase his type of milk (he can drink only soy).

"Did you put it on the list?" I asked.

"Mom, you knew we were out, so why should I have to put it on the list?"

Have you ever seen one of those cartoon moms who, when she gets really angry, steam starts to come out of her ears? Let's just say I could have heated two matching tea kettles at that point. That is when I gave Justen the lecture about the Magic List.

"That list you see on the fridge? That is a Magic List. As a teenager in this house, all you have to do is write down what you want and then somehow, magically, someone else will read that list, lovingly drive to the store, shop and pay for those items on the list, carry them inside, and put them away. All you have to do is write it down.

"At no other point in your life will you have a Magic List that you will not be responsible for. For the rest of your life you will be required to do all of those things for yourself. So, at this point, I would strongly suggest that you take full advantage of the Magic List and just WRITE DOWN WHAT YOU NEED AND STOP GIVING ME ATTITUDE."

There's that love of Jesus again…

If you don't have one already, hang a Magic List on your fridge and make the people of your house (who are of the age to get things out of the fridge without your consent) responsible for writing things down. If they want to have those items in the house again, they will learn. After I didn't pick up peanut butter for two weeks in a row (I don't eat it so I didn't put it on the list), my son remembered to put it on the list.

And for those of you who feel that it's a hopeless cause? Trust me. Justen has four items written down on the Magic List as I write this. There is hope.

Bulk Cooking

My motto? "If one is good, than six must be better." We do a lot of bulk cooking around this house. Whether it's freezer cooking our meals or making double batches of our favorite low-cal pumpkin muffins to freeze and eat on the run, I am a huge believer in making your cooking/baking efforts count. More on that in coming chapters.

Simpler Meals

On most nights, I am not looking to cook gourmet fare. I am looking for wholesome, delicious meals my family will eat.

When you start putting your ideas on paper for a month of meals, it's going to be easy to get swept away in all the beautiful recipes available to you. You may even be tempted by yummy side dishes and fun desserts.

Resist the temptation.

Don't do it.

Besides, some of my favorite meals to eat are the easiest to make. Don't make things harder on yourself. If you want a great reference for good simple meals, be sure to check out the *More-With-Less Cookbook* by Doris Janzen Longacre.

Stop Being a Short-Order Cook

Every family is different, and I'm not here to judge, but I have been amazed at the number of moms and dads who prepare four different meals for four different family members. Yes, I know about food allergies, and I really do believe there are just some foods that no one should be forced to eat. (I think after forty-plus years I can safely say I will never like green peppers.) However, for the most part, dinner should be an experience that brings us together.

Yes, we would occasionally cook pasta for the kiddos when we were having something more exotic, but it can be great fun to see your kids experiment with new food and try new things. I know it can also be a showdown. Fortunately, most kids do eventually outgrow their aversion to round food or whatever your kid won't eat this week.

I understand some families have a clean-your-plate policy, and I respect that. Our rule was, you had to try everything and you had to eat your veggies. I admit that when the kids were little I made an extra effort to make sure the vegetables were kid-accessible (chopped into small pieces, dipping sauces on the side).

But the idea of cooking separate meals for each family member may be one of the reasons it just seems easier to go through the Golden Arches—again. That's exactly what they will do for you (for a price).

I love the system that my friend Ruth put in place to get feedback from her kids:

> When I was a single mom with two boys, I liked to try out new recipes, but also wanted some feedback about the meals. On one occasion, my son Chris took a bite, scrunched his nose, and asked me if it looked like the picture in the cookbook. I don't even remember what I made, but he had an opinion, and my meal didn't look anything like he thought it should.
>
> Since then we've created a system for new recipes. First, they have to honestly tell me if they liked the food. Why or why not? What can be changed to make it better if they didn't like it? Should I make it again with discussed changes? Overall, what letter grade would they give it (A-F). We've tried so many new recipes with this system, and everyone knows that I'm not offended if they hate it. We've ordered pizza only once, because the food was awful.
>
> I save only the As unless a B can be fixed with our discussed changes and made into an A. It's taught both my boys to think outside the cookbook and not be afraid to experiment. Neither one of my boys will starve!

I love that Ruth asked for feedback, but I think valuing her kids opinions also taught them to be a little more adventurous in trying new foods.

Thaw a Night (or Two) Before

Using your freezer—and using it well—is one of the simplest ways to save time. If you're not waiting around for the microwave to defrost dinner, you can jump in quickly to meal preparation. At the beginning of the week, I take a look at what needs to be pulled out of the freezer. If it's a meal we're going to eat in the next four nights, I go ahead and put it in the fridge. Then, midweek, I will go freezer diving again to see what needs to be thawed for the rest of the week.

Make Two Meals at Once

It's Monday night and it's chicken taco night—olé! Take a look at your menu for the week and see what else you can prep for the meals to come. While you're shredding the chicken, could you shred enough for Wednesday night's chicken soup as well? Maybe you could wash and chop the veggies for tomorrow's stir-fry.

My favorite way of making two meals at once is to get the ingredients together for tomorrow's slow-cooker meal while I'm waiting for tonight's dinner to finish baking, simmering, or sautéing. I have a cooker with a removable pot (the only kind to have, in my opinion), so I just mix all the ingredients in the pot, place the lid over it, and put that in the fridge overnight. The next morning, all I have to do is put the pot back in the slow cooker and set it on low. When I get home, I'm greeted by my favorite smell—dinner!

Train Up a Child

There is a window of time in a kid's life where they want to help. Grating cheese is fascinating, mashing potatoes is fun, and mixing cake batter is off-the-charts exciting. Take advantage of your kid's enthusiasm, even if it won't be a huge time-saver in the beginning. Make sure you raise kids who are learning how to cook.

Although I work from home, there are times when I'm traveling, and I am so grateful that my kids learned how to make simple meals, early on. Now Justen will make food when his friends come over, and Kimber often offers to take over dinner prep if she knows I'm having a busy day. (Don't worry, I'm no super-parent. Her teenagerness comes out in other ways.)

The funny thing is, for the longest time I could barely get my boys to reheat a chicken nugget. Now that they're thinking about living on their own and have girls in their lives who they want to impress, Justen and Jeremy will often help out with the cooking chores. I consider it a modern-day miracle that all four of our kids, Roger, and I worked as a team to put on Christmas dinner this year. Now they all want to learn more—so I can sometimes sit back and just give direction.

A girl could get used to this.

Save Money

When Roger and I got married, we decided that I would pursue writing and speaking while being based out of our house so that our kids had someone to come home to. This decision did not come without a price.

No one goes into writing for the money. (OK, it has worked out well for J.K. Rowling, but she's the exception, not the rule.) Before, Roger had been the sole support for three people; now that number was jumping to six.

At first, while still in the honeymoon phase, we did a lot of eating out. It's easy to fall into bad habits when you're busy, but there's a price for all that convenience. Not only did our food budget expand, so did our waistlines.

About a year ago, Roger and I put ourselves on a one-month, eat-at-home challenge. Except for business meetings and my weekly Starbucks date with Justen, we ate only at home or packed food to eat out. Suddenly, we realized how much money we had been wasting on fast food and restaurant food. We have learned to eat at home more, but we are still fans of flavor and need to keep it interesting for ourselves and our kids.

So here is a short list of ways that we're working to keep our menus fun but affordable:

Clean Out the Cupboards Cooking

I take an inventory of what's lurking in our freezer, fridge, and pantry and see what magic I can concoct out of it. There's a great website called SuperCook.com where you can punch in the ingredients you have on hand, and it will suggest recipes for you to try. Make sure you take the website tour so you can use it to its full capacity.

Cook Our Own Chicken

It may seem obvious, but we were spending way too much on

precooked and shredded chicken for our salads, burritos, curries, etc. Now I just throw four frozen, boneless chicken breasts into a glass baking dish, cover it with foil, and bake for 45 minutes at 350 degrees. Once the breasts have cooled, I use my Pampered Chef Food Chopper to chop up the meat, and we throw that chopped up chicken into everything.

This also applies to other meats. As much as I love turkey on Thanksgiving, what I really love are the leftovers. After we have our requisite turkey-and-stuffing sandwiches for lunch on Friday, I package up the rest of the turkey for future use in stir-frys, casseroles, and curries. We actually prepare two turkeys at Thanksgiving—one smoked and one brined—to have a little variety and a lot of leftovers for us and our extended family.

Ham is another meat that I plan on leftovers. We will have our big meal with that spiral-cut ham, and then package up the leftovers for sandwiches, breakfast casseroles, and soups.

LeftOvers On Purpose

Whether it's making a double batch of turkey meatballs for spaghetti on Monday and Italian wedding soup on Wednesday, or making a huge batch of Roger's spaghetti sauce for dinner two nights in a row, planning for leftovers makes sense in both time and money. (More on creating LeftOvers On Purpose later.)

Shop Once a Week

Oh, it's so hard to force myself to plan the meals, see what ingredients we already have, and then shop for them, but oh, the money and time that I save! If I don't think ahead, I end up stopping by the store every other day and buying prepared foods that are more expensive and a waste of time, energy, and calories (and we end up eating at 7:45 at night). Even if I am determined to shop once a week, I usually have to make at least one extra trip for something essential that I forgot. But we've learned we can live without oranges for an extra two days, if need be.

Bulk Purchases

Yep, at first it is going to cost more. But in the not-so-long run, you are going to save time, money, and gas by having your everyday items at hand and ready to use. Here's a partial list of things we have bought in bulk over the past year:

- Oatmeal
- Apricots (we buy them from a local farmer and freeze them)
- Grass-fed beef
- Flour
- Spices
- Pasta
- Beans
- Cereal
- Rice
- Vanilla
- Coffee
- Canned goods
- Tuna
- Hard cheese (Parmesan, Romano)

We store our bulk purchases in airtight containers so they don't go bad. When our freezer gets low, we store some of the grains in there so that they take up space. It's more expensive to run an empty freezer than one packed with food.

Eat with the Seasons

If you buy strawberries in December, you're paying way more than you should. There really is a time for everything, and food is at the top of that seasonal list. Check out your local farmers' markets to see when's the best time of year to buy in your region, but here is a general guideline by season of some popular fruits and vegetables:

Winter

- Bell peppers
- Cabbage
- Celery
- Oranges
- Radishes

Spring

- Broccoli
- Carrots
- Spinach
- Strawberries
- Sweet potatoes
- Tomatoes

Summer

- Apples
- Greens
- Onions
- Nectarines
- Pears
- Watermelon

Fall

- Beets
- Squash
- Grapefruit
- Mushrooms
- Turnips

Eat Less Meat

I have been gradually reducing the amount of meat that goes into our dishes while trying to bulk up the veggies and alternate sources of protein (beans, meat-substitutes). Our goal for each meal is to have three-fourths of the plate be plants. We're not always successful (we won't even talk about the taquitos I had last night), but we're learning new cooking skills as we scale back on all things carnivore.

One of the ways we're tiptoeing into less meat eating is by gathering tried and true recipes from our favorite vegetarians. Here are a couple from my friend and fellow author Cheri Gregory that you can try:

• • • • • • • • • • **Walnut "Meat" Balls** • • • • • • • • • •

1 cup walnuts, finely chopped

1 cup Ritz crackers, crushed fine

1 cup cheddar cheese, shredded

3 eggs beaten

4-5 cups brown gravy

Mix all ingredients (except gravy) together and form into small balls (about the size of a large gumball.) Roll the balls in seasoned bread crumbs. Fry in a small amount of oil, turning 3 or 4 times until each side is golden brown.

Place meatballs in a casserole dish and pour the gravy over the meatballs. Bake at 350° 45 to 60 minutes.

• •

● ● ● ● ● ● ● ● ● ● ● ● ● **Lentil Loaf** ● ● ● ● ● ● ● ● ● ● ● ●

1 cup lentils, cooked and mashed

1½ cups Pepperidge Farms seasoned stuffing

2 beaten eggs

1 large can evaporated milk

½ cup walnuts, finely chopped

2 packages G. Washington's Golden Seasoning and Broth

½ cup oil

1 large onion, minced

Combine all ingredients and pour into greased loaf pan. Bake at 350° until browned and set, 45 to 60 minutes.

Note: This is fabulous on sandwiches. Just slice and slather on some catsup, cheese, avocado, lettuce, etc.

● ●

You are probably already eating meatless meals several times a week, but here are a few suggestions to consider: cheese quesadillas, peanut-butter-and-jelly sandwiches, veggie salads, vegetable soup, cheese and broccoli baked potatoes, oatmeal or other cereals for breakfast, bean burritos.

Waste Not: Co-op with Friends

When my kids were younger, I had a network of friends that would inform each other of sales at different supermarkets and, in some cases, would pick up sale items for each other. I'll never forget the time whole chickens were reduced to twenty-nine cents a pound at our grocery store, but I wasn't able to get there since I was babysitting a friend's kids. Her thank you? Mary brought me six whole chickens from the store. Best babysitting tip I've ever received.

This is also a good strategy for bulk purchases. Maybe you don't want a twenty-five-pound bag of flour sitting in your pantry, but dividing that flour with two friends suddenly makes the flour—and the price—more attractive.

If you are tight on space, co-oping with friends suddenly makes bulk purchases both affordable and manageable.

Learn to Cook from Scratch

OK, I want to be careful with this recommendation. I think cheating with prepared foods every once in a while is a fine idea. I don't want to give the impression that eating on the cheap is so difficult that the value meal at your favorite fast-food place looks more and more tempting. However, some things that are *so* expensive at the grocery store are surprisingly easy to prepare at home. Just some examples:

- Baked lasagna
- Mini pizzas (made with pita bread—so much better for you as well)
- Muffins
- Bread (especially if that bread maker from your wedding is gathering dust)
- Salad dressings
- Marinades

And be wary of that deli counter at your supermarket. Occasionally picking up a roasted chicken can be a lifesaver, but if you pick up four meals in a row and do your regular grocery shopping on top of that, you're wasting a lot of money.

Cut Your Own Veggies

Those packages of cut veggies are great if you're in a rush, but it's so much less expensive to cut your own. Don't get me wrong—I love a quick-and-easy bagged salad once in a while, but those tiny containers of chopped onions? You could buy a whole bag of onions for the same price.

Save Your Sanity

> *"I find that God made man simple; man's complex problems are of his own devising."*
>
> **ECCLESIASTES 7:30 (JERUSALEM BIBLE)**

Cook in Bulk

Some people are overwhelmed by the thought of bulk cooking, but to me, it's the simplest way to cook. We'll talk more about bulk cooking in chapter 11, "Freezer Cooking."

Stock a Pantry

Yes, having a pantry does save you time, money, and your sanity. There is nothing that makes me crazier than having all the ingredients for a recipe except for that one essential item. Having a pantry means I'm more likely to have on hand what I need—or at least some way to substitute for it.

Create Your Own Cookbook

Having all your recipes in a centralized place keeps you from having to hunt down that recipe for chicken cacciatore you downloaded off your friend's blog last week. I keep all the recipes I use regularly in a binder with clear sheet protectors. The recipes are organized by type—marinades, casseroles, BBQs, and so on—for easy retrieval and planning.

Prep Your Food

One of the biggest ways to keep my head above water in the kitchen is to put away my groceries well. My usual temptation is to just shove everything into place as soon as I walk through the door. However, if I take the time to prep the food that I can before it goes into the fridge, I'm going to have a whole lot less hassle when it comes to prepping dinner later on.

This has become even more critical now that our family is part of a farmers' co-op. Every Thursday I drive to my pick-up spot and tote back a bushelful of veggies and fruits for us to eat over the next week. If I don't prep those veggies right away, I'll probably have that same giant bag of greens staring me in the face the next Thursday as well.

Here are some things I do to prep the food from the store and the farmers' co-op as soon as I get home:

- Pull out my salad spinner and wash up all those greens.
- Wash all fruits and veggies that can be washed (have to wait to wash those strawberries until we're ready to eat them).
- Put all clean fruits and veggies in Debbie Meyer Green-Bags (bags that help your produce last longer).
- Shred cheese in the food processor.
- Divide up meat to be frozen. Bag and marinade.

Chapter 4

What Are You Going to Eat for 31 Days?

*"My mother's menu consisted
of two choices: Take it or leave it."*

BUDDY HACKETT

Plan out your meals for a month.

OK—let's all take a deep breath.

I know that for some of you, planning out your meals for four weeks is going to feel a little overwhelming. For some women, deciding what pair of jeans they're going to wear for running errands can feel like a huge decision. (Not for me. I pick whichever ones are clean...and fit.) Some of you may be thinking, *I don't even know what my life will be like in two weeks, how can I plan for it now?*

Exactly.

If you are like almost every other woman I know, life is super busy. Nobody I know is doing just one thing. If she's a stay-at-home mom, she's also leading her local MOPS group. If she's managing a houseful of teens, she's also managing her mobile accounting business on the side. If she's working full-time, she's also the head of the committee to raise funds for a well in a village in Africa.

And that's why I want you to have a plan.

I want what you and your tribe (family, roommate, friends) are having for dinner to be the least stressful decision of your day.

I want you to take a look at your calendar and your family's calendar, figure out what nights you can cook, when you can prep for meals later in the week, and what nights you need to have dinner waiting for you to get home. And then, I want you to sit down with your calendar and plan accordingly.

The Secret to Planning 31 Meals

For years, I have been taking a catch-as-catch-can approach to planning meals. I would sit down with a blank calendar and fill in the spots with meals I knew my family would like. I would make a shopping list based off of those ingredients, then go to the store and buy what I needed. I would go home with a plan in hand and the groceries to make it happen.

And that's when my plan would bump up against the reality of my life.

I would plan a stir-fry for Monday night. But no one was going to be home on Monday night—or at least not at the same time. My husband, Roger, would need to eat early because he has a phone call to India every Monday night. My son Justen works until after six o'clock. My daughter Kimber had drama rehearsal and didn't know when she would be home, and Jeremy, my stepson, was doing a drop in at 4:45 after school to change clothes for work.

Perhaps not the best night to do stir-fry?

Unless I wanted to be a short-order stir-fry cook (and let's be clear, I have no desire to do that), most of my people were not going to be able to eat dinner together (or at least not one they would want to eat).

It took me a while to figure out that Monday night in the Lipp-Hunter house was the perfect night for a big pot of soup and a yummy salad, something that was ready to serve at any of the o'clocks when my family members would be eating.

So now instead of planning what was for dinner, I was planning how I was going to cook dinner each night.

Taking all schedules into account (most importantly, the schedule of the person who was going to cook that day—and surprise, it's not always me!), I figured out what was going to be the best type of meal to fix.

Here are the meals I have to choose from:

Freezer Meals

These are meals I have prepared weeks or even months in advance and stick in the freezer to pull out at just the right time. Freezer meals are great for nights when I get home late. I can have someone else in my family stick the meal in the oven so it will be ready to go that evening. Or, when I'm extra organized, I can set the frozen meal in the oven in the morning and set the oven timer to turn on thirty to forty-five minutes before we want to eat. (I feel extra efficient when I do this. Kind of like Judy Jetson without the severe hairdo.)

Slow-Cooker Meals

I love my slow cooker—especially when I'm smart enough to pull all the ingredients together the night before. It gives me a warm fuzzy feeling to know that while I'm running around town doing errands or off working, my slow cooker is at home slaving away to have dinner ready for us when we get there. In part four of this book, I'll show you how to make freezer meals that you dump directly into the slow cooker so you can save yourself even more time and energy.

LeftOvers On Purpose (LOOP) Meals

I love this category because it feels like cheating. You had a balsamic pork roast for dinner on Tuesday, but your crew ate only half—and you're glad. You planned on cooking twice as much as you needed because those LeftOvers On Purpose are now being mixed together with bok choy, onions, and mushrooms to make an Asian stir-fry for Thursday night. (Please note: If you are making LeftOvers On Purpose, be sure to label your leftovers accordingly, especially if you have teenage boys in your home.)

Pantry Meals

The meat didn't defrost in time or it's the day before your grocery run and there's "no food in this house." Have no fear, pantry meals are here. Pantry meals are made primarily from ingredients you have on hand, adding in random ingredients you may have hanging around and want to use up. Leftover chicken or ground beef you hadn't planned on? Make a great chili from your pantry and throw in the meat—yum without waste. I usually plan one pantry meal at the end of the week, which is a great way to make sure that nothing goes to waste.

Fast Food at Home Meals

These are meals you actually cook that night. We all have our quick-and-easy family favorites that we couldn't live without. This is when I pull together a super-simple bowl of pasta with marinara, basil, and Parmesan cheese, a bagged salad and a couple of warmed-up croissants, or an Asian stir-fry. Each of us has our favorite go-to meals in this category.

Every Man for Himself Meals

We have this kind of meal about once a week. On nights when I'm working, everyone usually has to forage for themselves. This is an excellent way to use up leftovers, but I also make sure to keep on hand sandwich fixings for lunches and the EMFH nights.

Most of the dinners you see in this book fit under more than one category. That pasta dish I just mentioned under Fast Food at Home would also be considered a Pantry Meal. Call it what you will, just knowing you have a plan is going to make a world of difference.

The goal is to match the cooking method with your life—no stir-frys on soccer night, no freezer meals the night after you get home from the farmers' market, no pantry meals when you have tomatoes in your garden that you either need to use or lose. I want you to plan what you're going to eat around your life so that dinner is less mess and less stress.

Planning Your Meals

So here are the steps to getting your meal plan together:

1. Calendar. Go to www.ProjectsForYourSoul.com for a printable version of the Meal Planning Calendar.

2. Schedule. Look at the activities and schedules for those you are cooking for. Most households develop a weekly pattern over time. Tuesdays and Thursdays tend to be less chaotic around our house, Mondays everyone seems to work, and Wednesdays have always been a church night. Since we have teens and young adults at our house, Fridays are usually just Roger and me for dinner. And our big family dinners, when even the kids who don't live at home come back, are on Sunday evenings. While this schedule can vary wildly (especially when I'm traveling), it does have a basic flow that helps me plan my meals.

Once you have an idea of the schedule, write down the kind of meal you need to have that night. If you need to have dinner ready when you get home (and not worry about it burning in the oven), then a slow-cooker recipe could be the ticket for you.

So, following the above schedule, this is one way I could plan my meals for the week:

> *Sunday:* LeftOvers On Purpose, Round 1 (making enough ham, steak, chicken, etc. for Round 2 on Tuesday)
>
> *Monday:* Slow-Cooker Meal
>
> *Tuesday:* LeftOvers On Purpose, Round 2
>
> *Wednesday:* Freezer Meal
>
> *Thursday:* Fast Food at Home
>
> *Friday:* Every Man For Himself
>
> *Saturday:* Freezer Meal

3. Recipes. Now that you know *the type of meal* you should cook on a given night, it's time to figure out *what* to cook. Don't get overwhelmed! Start simple and small. Mix in one or two recipes from this book with your family's favorite recipes.

Besides your schedule, here are some other things to consider when making up your menus.

- *Time of year.* I like to eat seasonally as much as possible. If my garden is bursting with squash or the last time I went to the market the strawberries looked anemic (and were from a foreign country), those things influence my meal planning.

- *What I already have on hand.* When I hit a great sale on

chicken, I stock up. And my veggies from the farmers' market? Those babies have an expiration date. I want to be sensible with the food I purchase and use it before I lose it. So many times I have bought what I already had on hand because I didn't check first before making my meal plan and heading to the store.

- *The weather.* OK, this may not be the biggest consideration, but last year I put together a month's worth of meals for June without thinking once about barbecuing. Why have beef stew in the summer or Asian chicken salad in the dead of winter? Celebrate the seasons with delicious food.

So if I were to add some recipes to my meal plan, here is an idea of what one week of meals might look like:

Sunday: LeftOvers On Purpose, Round 1
Spice-rubbed pork roast with potatoes and ratatouille

Monday: Slow-Cooker Meal
Chili and bread-machine French bread with a
    blue cheese spring mix salad

Tuesday: LeftOvers On Purpose, Round 2
Left-over sliced pork with homemade mac-n-cheese
    and asparagus

Wednesday: Freezer Meal
Poppyseed chicken, bagged salad, and baked
    cinnamon apples

Thursday: Fast Food at Home
Veggie pita pizzas with turkey pepperoni

Friday: Every Man For Himself
Leftovers

Saturday: Freezer Meal
Teriyaki chicken with rice and grilled veggie kabobs

Try This at Home

Give yourself a week to plan and shop and do a little advance cooking for the freezer meals. Don't try to do the planning, shopping, and cooking all in the same day.

You may be one of those lucky people who shares the meal planning with someone else. If that's the case, I suggest for your first planning time that you set aside a good hour or so to go through the exercise. It actually is a lot of fun to do this with another person.

Part Two

Get Organized

Chapter 5

Solution 1—Organize Your Recipes

"I have a good collection of cookery books.
This is not so much because I like cooking,
but because I like eating."

LOUISE BROWN

Problem: I spend more time trying to figure out what to cook than actually cooking.

I love this story that was told to one of my friends, Robin Dilallo, by her grandmother:

> A woman was called to help care for a friend's children when the friend was called out of town suddenly with a family emergency. When she returned, the children raved about the woman's cooking and how she had made all their favorites.
>
> "However did you know what their favorites were?" the friend asked.
>
> "It was easy," the woman said. "I just looked for the recipes that had the most food stains on them."

How in the world are you going to have a heartwarming story like this if all your recipes are merely bookmarked on the Internet? Yes, I have the computer program to keep track of all my recipes, and I have my grandmother's recipe box. (Because she moved every year for ten years, each of her home addresses is written in pencil on the inside of the box, just so she could keep track of where she was living at any given moment.)

But I need a better way to preserve and keep track of all the gems I find—recipes copied at a friend's house after a particularly great meal; recipes found after a search of ingredients on the web; ideas clipped from the pages of magazines or the food section of the local paper.

As you navigate this adventure of preparing new and interesting meals for your family, it will be most important to keep track of all your successes. That's why I highly suggest a three-ring binder for all your cherished recipes. If you are already heavily invested in a computer or 3 x 5 card system, and it's working for you, great! However, if you just have fantasies of making it work, I strongly suggest you go to the binder system for several reasons:

- *It requires less paper.* You don't have to print out your recipe each and every time you use it.

- *It's easy to manage.* I just shove the new recipes into the front of the book until I'm cooking one day and have some time while I'm waiting for my marinara to simmer. That's when I'll grab my binder and start filing recipes.

- *It lets you make notes on the recipes.* That way, if you decide that your mushroom-and-chicken dish needs a little more garlic (and come on, what recipe couldn't use a little more garlic?), you don't have to boot up your computer to make the note on the recipe.

- *It's easy to use when planning your meals.* I can pull out the recipes I'm going to use for the week, month, whatever. I can have them all in one place for everything I'm cooking, whenever I'm cooking. It also makes creating a shopping list easier when I can flip through all my recipes and know that I'll need to stock up on chicken broth, crushed tomatoes, pasta, or whatever.

Create Your Own Cookbook

Ready? Here's how you can create your own cookbook:

BUY A THREE-RING BINDER AND SOME SHEET PROTECTORS.

It doesn't need to be a fancy binder, but I suggest a big one (three-inches thick that holds 8½ x 11 sheets) with a plastic cover that can be easily wiped clean. I also use tabbed page dividers to denote the different categories of recipes (more on that later).

SPEND SOME TIME GATHERING UP ALL YOUR RECIPES.

If you are like most women I know, you have recipes tucked away everywhere. It's time to pull all those recipes together in one place. Here are some arenas to explore for all those hidden treasures:

- Favorite recipe books
- Files on your computer
- Book-marked websites you visit
- Recipe boxes
- Kitchen drawers
- Church/school/community cookbooks
- Recipe cards from the grocery store

Once you have these all in one place, figure out how they're going to work in your new cookbook. Do you need to photocopy the recipes that are in books you own to put into your collection? (This is legal if you own the book and are copying it for your personal use.) Can you simply slip the 3 x 5 cards into sheet protectors to put in the binder? You may want all the recipes to look the same, typed out and formatted uniformly. If you really have to have all your recipes look the same, count on this taking several days. But here's the reality: I want you to spend your time cooking, not gearing up to cook. You could spend all your time making your cookbook look perfect and never cook a thing. What good would that be?

I love the mishmash of recipes in my book; it gives my binder a unique personality. I love looking at a recipe card in a sheet protector and knowing instantly it's my friend Shannon's world-famous recipe for artichoke dip, or seeing a notebook page with Japanese kanji on it and knowing that it contains my favorite recipe for apple bread saved from my year teaching English near Kyoto. Uniform pages may look organized, but I would rather have memories than uniformity anytime!

EDIT YOUR RECIPES.

Get rid of the recipes you are never going to use again. Back in the day, I made a dish from a cookbook recipe that sounded delicious: warm turkey-meatball salad with a lemon dressing. While the meatballs were frying in a pan, I copied the recipe onto a notebook page for future reference. Once we sat down to eat, it became clear there was no need for a future reference—the salad was terrible! But for some reason, I held on to that recipe for another six years. Why? Get rid of all those recipes that are:

- Not redeemable
- Don't fit your lifestyle
- Duplicates

SLIP YOUR RECIPES INTO SHEET PROTECTORS.

I love having my recipes in sheet protectors—it makes them easy to clean when some wayward tomato sauce splatters on them, and easier to file. Even if they are on 3 x 5 cards, I can just slip them into a sheet protector and I'm ready to go.

ORGANIZE YOUR RECIPES.

Most recipes are organized by types of foods: chicken dishes, beef dishes, casseroles, and so on. I do it a bit differently. My recipes are organized by how the dish is prepared: slow-cooker meals, freezer meals, quick fix meals (such as stir-fry), and LeftOvers On Purpose (LOOP) meals. Additionally, I have a general category for other types of meals.

I advise you to organize your recipes in a way that makes sense to you. If you want to stick with the traditional "chicken, beef" categories, that's great. As long as it's a system that works for you, that's what matters. If you want to give my way a try, here's what I do:

I have a generous supply of page protectors at hand and dedicate a page divider to each of my major categories:

- Slow-cooker Meals
- Freezer Meals
- Fast Food at Home Meals
- LOOP Meals
- Microwave cooking
- BBQ
- Pressure cooker

Some other recipe categories are for things that not related to dinner, but I need a safe place to keep these recipes as well:

- Baking
- Desserts
- Side dishes

Within each of those categories, I figure out what my major categories are and make tabs for those. For instance, under "Freezer Meals" I have tabs for "Chicken Casseroles," "Beef Casseroles," "Marinades," and "Miscellaneous." It just makes it that much easier to retrieve my recipes quickly and efficiently.

Ready for more good news? You will have to do only one major setup! After that, the system will all but maintain itself. About once a month, I review and file recipes I've found and want to try, or take out recipes that we've tried and no longer like. This works for me, and I believe it will work for you too.

I love this system because it allows me to play around with the recipes I choose. This is especially helpful when I'm trying to create menu plans, major cooking days, or shopping lists. And when I'm cooking, I either clip my recipe to a magnet on the side of my fridge or tape it to my kitchen cabinet using blue painter's tape (so as to not leave a mark). You can't do that with a recipe on the Internet!

Other Cookbooks

Yes, I do keep some other cookbooks on my shelf. Here's a list of the ones that I hold on to:

- A basic cookbook (such as *Betty Crocker Cookbook*, *Better*

Homes and Gardens Cookbook, or *Joy of Cooking,*) so if I want to experiment, I have a number of basic recipes I can tweak.

- *More-With-Less Cookbook* by Doris Janzen Longacre. This has hundreds of useful recipes, tips, and ideas.

- A vegetarian cookbook. When I get my farmers' market produce, this has recipes for vegetables I normally don't buy.

- A basic slow-cooker recipe book. If I'm getting creative with a new recipe, I can find a similar one to compare cooking time with.

- Specialty cookbooks such as:
  - A cheese-making cookbook
  - Regional cookbooks
  - Church cookbooks (mostly for the memories)

And what if you are among the 1 percent of people who have a fabulously organized recipe system? After the glow of superiority has waned (really, I'm not judging—you've earned it), you have my permission to make a splash with a nifty new cookbook. Go on, you deserve it!

Try This at Home

Set aside a couple of nights for watching TV and creating your cookbook. This is a great project (little or huge, depending on how many recipes you have and want to keep) to do while catching up on all your TiVo-ed shows. Just remember—the way to make this project go faster is to edit, edit, edit. Get rid of the recipes you will never use. In the long run, it will make your job easier.

Or as a Group

Organizing your cookbooks would make an excellent group get-together with neighbors, a MOPS group, coworkers, or any group of women who want to be more organized. Led by you (or your most organized friend), gather together some sheet protectors, binders, file tabs, and a copy machine, and go to town getting all your recipes organized.

Guests could also bring copies of favorite recipes to exchange. By bringing one copy for each person, you'll go home with the same number of copies of different recipes. You could even turn this into a potluck extravaganza with each person bringing a favorite dish to share along with its recipe.

Organizing is so much more fun when food is involved.

Chapter 6

Solution 2—Organize Your Space

*"Organizing is what you do before you do something,
so that when you do it, it is not all mixed up."*

A.A. MILNE

> **Problem:** I would cook if I could find anything in my kitchen. Every time I go to make dinner, it turns into a game of hide-and-seek with my tools and ingredients.

If you are like most homemakers in America, your kitchen is stocked and ready for action. You have every modern convenience, and even a few to spare. You have pots and pans, a microwave (or two), a food processor, a Crock-Pot, and everything else that you need to make gourmet meals every single night.

So why is it so tempting to hit the deli counter at the supermarket when it comes to dinner? Is it because you haven't set up your kitchen for the type of work you need to be doing?

- Do you have to clear off your counters every time you want to fix a sandwich?

- Is it a game of hide-and-seek every time someone else in your family unloads the dishwasher?

- Do you have to move two pots and three pans to get to the baking dish you want?

You are going to spend more of your life cooking than doing almost any other activity besides sleeping and working, so why not make your kitchen as usable—and pleasant—as possible.

Reclaim Some Counter Space

The most valuable real estate in your entire house is the space on your counter. There should be nothing on the counter that doesn't either: (1) work regularly for you, or (2) make you happy when you look at it. My coffeemaker sees more action than the funnel-cake stand at a county fair, so it deserves a place on the counter. I use my food processor only once a week or so. It has not earned the right to be on the counter.

I have to fight regularly with my stuff to keep it off the counter. I promise you, clutter and appliances migrate there in the middle of the night. I am constantly waging a battle to keep my counters cleared.

Here's a list of things that have not earned the right to be there (but keep trying to sneak their way on):

- Slow cooker
- Can opener
- Kids' school projects
- Dishes that just don't want to get put away
- Mail

Things that have earned the right to be on my counter:

- Coffeemaker
- Canisters (they are not just decorative, they hold everyday essentials like coffee filters, packets of sweetener, and dog treats)
- Toaster oven (so we don't need to fire up the big oven very often)
- Spices
- A container of frequently used utensils
- A butcher block of knives
- Toaster

Your use of counter space is going to be different from mine, but you get the idea—be thoughtful about what you allow to live on your counter.

Another great counter space saver is to see what you can have mounted under your cabinets or on your walls. For the longest time, I had a vertical paper towel rack that sat on the counter. It was a constant frustration to me that it took up so much space. Then one day it occurred to me that just because our house wasn't built with an under-counter towel rack didn't mean I couldn't do the job myself (or bribe my cute husband to do it with a plateful of chocolate-chip cookies). I also have a microwave and CD player/radio mounted under my cabinets to save space.

And on my walls? I have a very cute set of stainless-steel measuring spoons and a coffee scoop. I use them every day, they look great on the walls, and everyone in my house knows where to put them away. Another space-saving idea I've seen is a magnetic knife holder mounted on the wall.

I'm sure as you look around your kitchen or browse in a kitchen gadgets store, you'll think of other creative ways to clear your counters.

Edit Your Cabinets

It's easy to let pots and pans multiply in those dark spaces. I have a tiny kitchen, so I've had to become ruthless in what gets to stay.

I think many people stock their kitchens for major holidays, keeping six casserole dishes in their cabinets because that's what they use on Easter, or keeping the turkey roaster in a main cabinet even though they roast a turkey only every other year.

I suggest you get rid of as much stuff as possible. Keep a few pots, pans, and casserole dishes that you use every day in your cabinets, and then store the stuff that you use only a couple of times a year out of sight. Use a big storage bin for those extras and bring the tub in for holidays. When you're cleaning up from having the extended family over for Grandma's birthday, just wash those extra pots and pans and put them in the tub. Under no circumstances let them back into your cabinets.

Since we have limited cabinet space, I've had to get extremely creative with where we put stuff. I have a large butcher-block island in the middle of our kitchen with two giant baskets on the bottom shelf. In one basket I store all my cooking pots; in the other basket, all my kitchen towels, cloth napkins, and pot holders. In the extra room on that shelf, I store my rice cooker and my slow cooker (both of which I use once or twice a week).

Another way we created space in the kitchen-dining area was to use a pullout bench with a storage drawer underneath as seating in our dining room. The storage drawer has plenty of room for some larger appliances (standing mixer, food processor) and the bench looks great with a couple of pillows thrown on top of it.

Though I don't have a large kitchen (and just thinking about the lack of cupboard space can make me spontaneously weep), some of my friends have downright tiny spaces. Here's what they have done to make their "efficiency kitchens" actually efficient.

FROM MARTHA ORLANDO IN GEORGIA:

"Here are a few things that we have done in our kitchen that have turned a rather small space into an amazingly functional area. (My hubby, Mr. Engineer, does most of the cooking, so I have to give him credit here. I do the baking.)

- Small lazy Susan inside a cabinet for our spices
- Canisters with cooking utensils on the counter
- Two overhead racks for pots, pans, and colanders
- Hooks on the walls for strainers, funnels, measuring cups and spoons
- Portable island with extra cabinet space, built-in knife block, and paper-towel rack; it serves as both prep space and seats two on stools if we have extra company."

FROM RUTH SHAVE IN ARIZONA:

"Think outside the usual storage places. We have a very funky-shaped pantry in our kitchen with *lots* of wasted space...way up high. I had my husband, Kevin, build shelves all the way to the ceiling so I can store the roasting pan, canner, extra paper towels, and other stuff I don't need every day but don't want to store in the hot garage.

"We found another hidden space inside the same pantry. Above the door, Kevin nailed a strip of wood and mounted hooks on it. I hang the huge soup ladle I use every few months, my fine-mesh sieves that kept falling out of the cabinet, etc. I know exactly where they are, they are easy for me to get to, and they don't take up valuable space.

"Spend some time in an IKEA store or on their website. They are fabulous at utilizing small spaces effectively. One trip through and we had lots of ideas on how to use the way-up-high spaces."

Fresh Start with Fresh Food

Take some time to clean out your expired and "I'm never going to use this" food. Pitch what is expired and donate what is usable. Check with your local food bank to find out what they are looking for.

When you don't have to wade through never opened jars of wasabi mustard and bags of soy chips that your health-nut friend insisted you buy, you can get down to the business of cooking.

Don't stop at your fridge and food cabinets. Go through your freezer, and anything you can't identify, pitch. Anything you can't remember putting in there, pitch. If you can't imagine yourself eating it in the next week, pitch it.

Keep going. What about those spices that you bought to make jambalaya three years ago. If you're never going to use them again, get rid of them. (And after three years, they're starting to lose their flavor anyway.)

Keep It Hip

Make sure that your kitchen is a place where you want to hang out. I love my kitchen. It isn't anything that would end up in *House Beautiful*, but it's clean, warm, friendly, and functional. Make sure that your kitchen greets you well.

- Hang up some artwork—even if it's small—that makes you smile.

- I have a set of iPod speakers in the kitchen, so while I'm working I can also listen to some worship music (or, if I need an extra boost of energy, the B52s).

- For our first anniversary, Roger made me a simple window box with a small ledge for tealight candles. The color of the box is the same warm, golden yellow as the interior paint of my kitchen. I make sure there's something pretty and living in that window box year round. (I live in California, so that's actually possible here.)

- Every couple of years I go crazy and get new kitchen towels. I know several moms who buy their kids the latest clothes at Gap Kids but are using kitchen towels from the eighties. Time to splurge (and by splurge, I mean twenty dollars or so at Target). My kitchen towels become my cleaning towels and my cleaning towels become the garage towels and the garage towels become recycling. Circle of life, baby.

Try This at Home

1. In your kitchen, set up three cardboard boxes and one large plastic storage tub, a garbage bag, and a recycle bag (for any empty boxes or cans that can go straight into your recycling bin), your iPod, and a timer (you can use the one on your cell phone or your oven).

2. Mark one cardboard box "Goodwill," one "Food Donations," and one "Put Away."

3. Give yourself fifteen minutes on your timer and pick a cabinet.

4. Start picking through the cabinet and use the three boxes to sort the contents. If you have too many mugs, donate what you can't use to Goodwill or any other organization you find worthy. We keep only the mugs we truly love— mugs have to earn the right to remain in our cabinets. Any edible food you won't use right away and that fits the

food-bank donations guidelines gets put in the "Food Donations" box. Anything that's out of place ("Why is there a baby sock on the dog-food cabinet?") is put in the "Put Away" box.

5. Oh, and let's be clear: don't donate garbage; put it in the garbage bag. It costs charities time and money to get rid of stuff that you don't want—and nobody else wants either. Donate only those things that are in decent condition and are worthy of reselling.

6. Finally, any of your pots, pans, dishes, or tablecloths that you use only during the holidays get put in the plastic tub. I am a bit of a holiday nut, so I have several plastic bins, one for each holiday (OK, six for Christmas). But I have one big tub that's just for those serving platters and roasting pans that come out only once or twice a year. If you have a giant kitchen, don't worry about this. But if, like most of us, your kitchen feels more like a ship's galley, this can free up a bunch of space.

If this project feels totally overwhelming to you, consider having a supportive friend or someone you hire follow these guidelines for you. There is a lot of freedom in a fresh start.

"I just paid an organizer to do pretty much what you outlined," one of my blog readers said. "But I have so many emotional and physical stresses right now that I was unable to even think about what goes where. Now—I just sit and look at my clean counters and clean kitchen. I feel like I'm ready to cook, and cook *almost* anything!"

And when you're done? Reward yourself with some new kitchen towels, pot holders, or a great plant (that doesn't have to sit on your counter).

I want to make sure that your kitchen doesn't defeat you before you even get started. Keep what's best and get rid of the rest.

Or as a Group

If you are going through *The "What's for Dinner?" Solution* as a group, set a date to clean out your cabinets, and then bring the left-overs to your next gathering. Maybe someone else is dying to have the deviled-egg plate you got as a gift from your great aunt. One group even did a garage sale with all their kitchen leftovers (plus assorted baby items) to help pay for childcare for that month's meeting.

Chapter 7

Solution 3—Organize Your Tools

"And I find chopsticks frankly distressing. Am I alone in thinking it odd that a people ingenious enough to invent paper, gunpowder, kites and any number of other useful objects, and who have a noble history extending back 3,000 years, haven't yet worked out that a pair of knitting needles is no way to capture food?"

BILL BRYSON

Problem: I have twelve cookie sheets but no can opener. I never have the right stuff to make the recipes I want.

Dust off your Crock-Pot and grab some Ziploc bags. It's time to get prepared for some serious cooking.

Before I garden each spring, I spend some time making an inventory of the things I have and what I need in order to get digging. Of course I know I'll need new plants, but what about all those other little things that I don't think about until I am elbow deep in Miracle-Gro Potting Mix? I hate having to stop and run to the garden store because I ran out of pots or didn't have enough tomato stakes. Now I keep in the garage a list of everything I might need so when my green thumb starts to itch on the first clear day of spring, I'm ready for action.

It's the same before a big cooking day. I usually dedicate one day a month to get ahead on all my cooking chores—dividing, marinating, and freezing those large packages of meat from the warehouse store; mixing up marinades to use right away as well as to freeze; cooking up pasta for some frozen casseroles; baking chicken breast to shred for salads and casseroles; washing and cutting up veggies for the coming week's meals; and generally just organizing the kitchen for the coming month.

Get-Ready Resources

So that you have on hand all the tools you'll need for a big cooking day, or even just for getting your curry on the table for Thursday's dinner, here's my list of get-ready resources. Of course, adjust for what you'll actually use and what you already have on hand.

Knives

- 3- or 4-inch paring knife
- a serrated knife
- 8- or 10-inch chef's knife

Measuring Cups and Spoons

- ¼ cup through 1 cup in metal or plastic (I suggest getting two sets for extreme cooking.)
- glass measuring cup with spout for liquids (I have a 4-cup glass measuring cup I use for marinades all the time.)

Spoons and Mixing Utensils

- slotted spoon
- wooden spoons
- sturdy metal spoons
- soup ladle
- handheld electric mixer
- wire whisks in different sizes

(I have a set of measured serving spoons from Weight Watchers that I love. That way, when my diet says "a cup of brown rice," I can actually serve myself a cup of rice.)

Spatulas

- straight spatulas
- angled-handle spatulas
- rubber-scraper spatulas

Pots and Pans
- different-sized saucepans with lids
- 12-inch skillet with cover
- 6- or 8-inch nonstick skillet
- roasting pan
- 9 x 13 baking pan
- cooling racks
- two cookie sheets

Kitchen Equipment
- slow cooker (I have a 6-quart and a 4-quart.)
- freezer (with room in it!)

Miscellaneous
- potato peeler
- cutting board (I have one for meats and one for veggies and breads in two different colors so I don't cross contaminate.)
- grater
- can opener (electric or manual)
- probe digital meat thermometer
- colander
- freezer bags (I use the gallon and two-gallon variety for 9 x 9 pans and 9 x 13 pans, respectively.)
- zip-style sandwich bags
- cling wrap
- aluminum foil

As you grow in your kitchen wisdom, you'll know what gadgets are fluff and what's the right stuff. In my experience, almost anything that's "As Seen on TV" (except for the Debbie Meyer GreenBags for keeping fruits and veggies fresh longer) is probably not worth the money or the kitchen space.

Some Nonbasic Resources

I do have a few other suggestions for some nonbasics that I've gathered over the years:

- *A seasoned black-iron skillet.* I don't know why, but food out of these just tastes better.

- *An apple peeler/corer/slicer.* I make a lot of fruit and oatmeal bakes and cobblers for a healthy dessert, and this little gadget cuts the prep time by 75 percent.

- *A standing mixer.* Yes, it's an investment, but once you can afford it you will never go back.

- *A rice cooker.* One of the simplest appliances I've ever owned. Mine is twenty years old and makes perfect rice every time. Just click it on and forget it.

Each person will have her own list of "Musts." While my friend Ruth believes in having a simple kitchen, she has a few things she can't live without:

> You really can cook a great meal (or many!) with just the basics. Think of what the pioneer women had for cooking tools. I can envision them crossing the United States in their covered wagons and getting to a large river and having to leave things behind in order to get the wagon across. If that were me, I would have a tough time deciding what to leave. I could see myself tying my rolling pin, my measuring cups, my spoons, and my other "must haves" to the lining of my pioneer skirt and swimming to the other side!

I've probably used a rolling pin twice in the past five years. Each cook is different. You have to come up with what works for you, and then buy the best you can afford.

Try This at Home

Now don't panic! While the things on the get-ready list are considered basics, you may not have them all. That's OK. Read through your recipes to see what will be required—and then improvise. I usually find that it's not the lack of equipment in my kitchen; it's having so much equipment that I can't get to what I need.

However, if you didn't have that wedding shower where you got four covered casserole dishes, you may be missing a few items. Here are some suggestions for rounding out your tool set if you're creating a kitchen on a dime:

Ask your mom. If you have that kind of relationship with your mom (and thankfully, I do), ask her if she has a slow cooker she's not using or a whisk that's no longer needed. I have a box of "extra stuff" set aside for whenever the first of my kids moves out on their own (into something other than a dorm room where even a hot plate is verboten). If your mom is like most moms in America, she probably has more stuff than she can use and would love to know it's going to be used and loved.

Go to a secondhand shop. When I've moved over the years, I have donated some perfectly good kitchenware to Goodwill and similar places.

Hit some garage sales. I found a stainless-steel bowl set and a colander at a moving sale for breathtakingly cheap. Call me calculating, but I like to go to upper-middle-class neighborhoods for their garage sales and hope to find a chronic upgrader who wants the newest and latest gadgets. They are looking to get rid of last year's models for fast cash—and there I am with my roll of dollar bills waiting for their castoffs.

Be patient. So you may not have a probe digital thermometer lying around—it's not a necessity. (However, I must say the number of dried-out roasts I've served since I got one has gone down significantly.) Start keeping a list of the things you still want or need. I've put several things on my birthday/Christmas/Mother's Day lists. I do get asked upon occasion what I would like for a gift, and it's nice to have something to say besides, "A gift card always works."

Become a member of Freecycle. Join your local Freecycle group (www.freecycle.org) and post what you need for your kitchen. I have a friend who furnished her whole kitchen (and most of her living room) this way. All you do is post the item you're looking for, and then wait for someone to contact you and say, "Why yes, I do have an extra garlic press! Here are the directions to my house." I love when I can meet someone's specific need through Freecycle.

Borrow. For years, when I would do a big cooking day, I would borrow my mom's food processor to do my chopping for me. It was worth the forty-minute round-trip to avoid chopping all those onions by hand. Borrow what you need to make it easier. And of course, be willing to lend as well.

Just buy it. Not to be the cause of any marital strife here, but I always find it funny that it's perfectly OK for a man to purchase a top-of-the-line saw for hundreds of dollars, but we feel weird about buying decent-quality kitchen equipment. And I would venture to guess that in most households, the medium-quality nonstick skillet will be used ten times as often as that saw.

When Roger and I were dating, I would go to his house to make dinner. Let me just say the conditions were less than ideal. His knives were so dull that kindergarten classes could have used them during craft time with no worries of the kids nicking themselves. He had one giant measuring cup and one giant cutting board and no wooden spoons. It was like cooking on the island of *Lost* without the rations from the airplane. But, I made it work—and so can you. (And trust me, you will appreciate that digital meat thermometer so much more if you have to wait for it.)

Or as a Group

If you are doing *The "What's for Dinner?" Solution* as a group, consider a kitchen swap. Everyone brings tools they're not using and swaps them for what they do need. I have done this casually with friends (we made a night out of it with everyone bringing appetizers), or you could do it as a Bible study or mother's group.

Another approach is to let others in your group know what you would be willing to lend. Do you have a large slow cooker someone could use for a big cooking day? Or how about a Seal-a-Meal you could loan, while they provide their own bags. There is no need for everyone in your group to own every piece of equipment—as long as you're willing to set a good example for your kids and share your toys.

Chapter 8

Solution 4—Organize Your Pantry

"Even the most resourceful housewife cannot create miracles from a rice-less pantry"

CHINESE PROVERB

Problem: I feel like every time I want to cook something, it means another trip to the grocery store. *Ugh.*

Why Everyone Needs a Pantry *(or, How Mother's Day Could Have Gone Horribly Wrong)*

It was Sunday at 1:00 in the afternoon, and I said to Roger, "I guess we better figure out what we're having for Mother's Day lunch."

Normally, I do plan a bit more in advance when my mom and dad are coming over, but it had been a crazy weekend. Roger and I had traveled out of town so I could speak at a church on Saturday, and then came right home so I could do the sermon for both services the next day at our church.

Fortunately, I had picked up a large ham at the warehouse store earlier in the week, and my friend Nancy had bought me a cake for Mother's Day, so the main dish and dessert were taken care of. Score!

Now—to round out the rest of the meal. In an hour.

I started to rummage through the freezer: frozen turkey meatballs. The fridge: a bag of salad, some low-fat ricotta and fat-free cream cheese. Oh, and half a dozen potatoes and some pita pockets. All stuff I usually keep on hand. Doesn't sound very exciting, does it?

This is where my culinary *MacGyver* skills were put to the test. All I needed was a paperclip, some chewing gum, and my pantry.

75

Here are the pantry-friendly recipes that I used to round out our Mother's Day meal:

● ● ● ● ● ● ● ● ● **Chipotle Apricot Meatballs** ● ● ● ● ● ● ● ● ●

1 small package of frozen turkey meatballs

1 jar apricot preserves (pantry)

1 bottle chipotle BBQ sauce (pantry)

Place all ingredients in a medium saucepan and bring to a boil. Turn the heat down and simmer for 20 minutes until meatballs are heated through.

Serves 8 as an appetizer.

● ●

● ● ● ● ● ● ● ● ● ● ● **Artichoke Dip** ● ● ● ● ● ● ● ● ● ● ● ●

8 oz. cream cheese

1 cup Parmesan cheese, shredded

1 cup mayonnaise (low-fat or fat-free is acceptable) (pantry)

½ tsp. dill weed

1 clove garlic, crushed

1 can artichoke hearts, drained and chopped (pantry)

Preheat oven to 350°. Cream the cream cheese, add the Parmesan cheese, mayonnaise, dill weed, and garlic. Mix well. Fold in the chopped artichoke hearts and then spoon mixture into a 9 x 9 pan. Bake for 30 minutes. Serve with crackers, toasted baguettes, or toasted pita points. Serves 8 as an appetizer.

● ●

● ● ● ● ● ● ● ● ● ● **Toasted Pita Points** ● ● ● ● ● ● ● ● ● ●

4 pitas

¼ cup extra-light virgin olive oil (pantry)

¼ cup Parmesan cheese

Using a pizza cutter, cut each pita into eight pie-shaped wedges. Brush on olive oil and sprinkle with Parmesan cheese. Put under broiler until the cheese is golden brown. Serves 8 as an appetizer.

● ● ● ● ● ● ● ● ● ● **Ricotta Mashed Potatoes** ● ● ● ● ● ● ● ● ●

Approximately 6 large russet potatoes, peeled and cut into quarters

¼ cup ricotta cheese

salt and pepper to taste

Place potatoes and enough water to cover in large pot. Bring to a boil. Reduce heat to medium and cook for approximately 15 to 20 minutes or until potatoes are tender. Drain potatoes well. Place potatoes back in pot and add cheese, salt, and pepper. Mash using handheld masher until smooth.

Serves 4 to 8.

With the ham in the oven, I started on the artichoke dip so that my guests could have something to munch on while lunch finished up in the oven. After I mixed up the ingredients, I placed the artichoke dip in the toaster oven I keep on the counter. While that was cooking, I dumped all of my ingredients for the apricot chipotle meatballs into the pot.

Meanwhile, Roger was peeling potatoes to be boiled And the kids? Doing the dash-and-stash cleaning system, sweeping the floor, and setting the table. After years of grandparent visits, they have the routine down.

I put the appetizers and plates on the butcher block, ripped open the bag of salad, and dinner was served.

I love to plan out meals for guests, but it's also great to know that even though I was short on time this weekend, we could have a real "make it work" kind of meal all because of a well-stocked pantry.

(By the way, Roger wants you to know that he took me out for sushi that night, bought me two gifts, and made sure that all our offspring suitably recognized me on the Mother of all Holidays. He was concerned that I was giving the impression that I was forced to cook my own Mother's Day meal.)

Pantry Basics

First off, let me tell you what I consider a pantry. A pantry is shelving space where someone keeps a back stock of nonperishable foods and ingredients for recipes.

Why Have a Pantry?

The best argument for having a pantry is to save both *time* and *money*.

- I can stock up on loss-leader items at the supermarket.
- I can use coupons to purchase multiple items.
- I can buy in bulk at Costco.
- I save precious shelf space in my kitchen.
- I save trips to the store by shopping in the pantry.
- When there is a need in the community, I have well-priced food I can donate.
- When the power goes off, we have a hand-operated can opener, a BBQ grill, a pot, and a pantry full of food we can get creative with (this has helped us more than once).
- When we've had friends in a financial crisis, we've been able to invite them to shop our pantry.
- When we've had lean financial months, it's great to know there's a back stock of food to pull from.

SOME REASONS MY FRIENDS CONSIDER A PANTRY ESSENTIAL:

"The benefits of having a pantry while living in the mountains are critical. Our closest milk is twenty minutes away, so we have to have extra of everything. If you were to look in my pantry, you would think we were squirrels!"—Jane Liddle

"If I keep things in my pantry, there is less running to the store last minute, and if I have meat in my freezer and a vegetable in the fridge, I am happy."—Gwen Stevenson

"We have a large pantry in our kitchen where we keep most of the canned goods, cereal, spices, pasta, sugar, etc. We have a small kitchen with few cabinets, so all food goes in the pantry. We do most of our shopping at Costco because it has the best prices, and we live forty minutes from town. We have a wired shelving unit in the garage that has five shelves, and we keep all of our big bulk items there."—Niki Kashner

"We have an overflow area in our office for snack items and cereal. This annoys the tar out of my hubby, but when I can get the cereal that we love for $0.50 for a $4 box, why not buy a few? When you coupon, you must have a pantry or stockpile location, no matter how crude the setup. You don't want all your scores sitting on your kitchen counter! I love shopping my pantry or stockpile—it saves us money since I got everything at a major discount and saves me from having to run to the store."—Angela Hood

"I hate being in the middle of a recipe and running out of stuff! So, in my pantry/kitchen/under the kids' beds, I have at least one unopened container of everything I use."—Robin Anderson

Where to Put a Pantry?

Some houses (usually really, *really* old or really, *really* new) come with a pantry space. For the rest of us living in homes built since TV was invented and after *Friends* went off the air, we need to get creative with where our pantry will go.

The two main things to think about when creating a pantry are *cool* and *dry*. You don't want to be close to any moisture or in a place where the temperature varies dramatically.

My pantry is a tiny corner of my garage where I have three bookcases I salvaged from a friend's junk pile. They are arranged in a U and hold all my pantry food items. In a previous house, the owners before us were clever enough to install their original cabinets in the garage when they remodeled their kitchen.

Here in California I don't know too many people with basements, but in the Midwest I know several friends who have put in shelving downstairs to create a pantry.

If you have a larger home without a designated pantry, see if you can repurpose an underused area as one of my readers did:

"Since our house does not have a food pantry, we had to use one of the kitchen cabinets for our food, and nothing much fit in it. We now use a former linen closet next to the formal dining room as our pantry."—Linda Jenkins

In one of our first apartments, I stored extra food items in the baby's room. Our son didn't take up much room at the time, and neither did his stuff. (Oh, and if having that pantry could save me one trip to the store a month with a six-month-old? So worth it.)

I have heard of some apartment dwellers using the space under their beds to store some canned goods.

Here's another creative way one of my readers made a pantry where there wasn't one:

"We don't have a pantry, but our kitchen is large enough that I've been able to place some large shelves in the kitchen without blocking much floor space. I have cereal and boxed food on the top two shelves, canned fruit on the middle shelf, canned veggies on the next shelf, and the bottom shelf holds things like salad dressing, pasta sauce, and BBQ sauce. I have a couple of small shelves next to that that hold my cookbooks and baby formula and baby food."—Rachel Davis

What Do You Keep in Your Pantry?

First, *large bulk packages that I refill from*. For example, I buy rice in bulk and store it in a big tub. I then refill my smaller container that

I keep in the kitchen from my tub of rice in my pantry. I do this with bulk purchases. Here's a list of those items in my pantry. Your list will differ due to the food needs in your family, but you get the general idea:

- Spices bought in large bottles
- Flour
- Oatmeal
- White sugar
- Rice
- Cold cereal
- Olive oil
- Soy sauce
- Vinegar
- Dry dog food
- Dry cat food

Second, *stuff that is unopened.* These are things that come in smaller packages, but I use them frequently and don't want to run out of them:

- Canned diced tomatoes
- Canned tomato paste
- Canned stewed tomatoes
- Pasta sauce
- Pasta
- Cornmeal
- Brown sugar
- Pinto beans
- Corn starch
- Chicken broth
- Vanilla
- Peanut butter
- Microwave popcorn
- Canned fruits and veggies
- Canned soups
- Catsup
- Mayonnaise
- Mustards
- Pickles
- Relish
- Tuna
- Canned chicken
- Sauces (BBQ, curry, marinades)
- Cling wrap
- Aluminum foil
- Gallon freezer bags
- Sandwich bags
- Cleaning supplies

Again, this is not a comprehensive list, but it gives you an idea of items that work in a pantry. Any items that are open (the jar of peanut butter currently in use, the box of crackers we opened last week) are in the kitchen cupboards. This reminds me to use those up first.

A helpful exercise is to go through your recipes and see what items you use regularly. If you use tuna only once a month for a salad you take to potlucks, there's no need to devote pantry space to tuna. If, however, you live with my son Justen, who makes himself a tuna sandwich every other day, stocking up on tuna is a must.

Storage Pantry-style

Food storage is so important, especially for pantries in the garage or basement. Be sure any bulk items that are opened are stored in airtight containers. This is especially important with grains such as flour and rice.

Not to freak anyone out, but I put any large bags of grains in the freezer overnight before storing them in the pantry in order to kill off any "wee beasties" that may have taken up residence. Some of those grains have made long trips from their growing point and have picked up some hitchhikers along the way.

Once I have the big bags stored in labeled containers in the pantry, I just refill the smaller containers from the kitchen.

Don't Let the Pantry Defeat You

When I asked my friends and readers how they felt about their pantries, most waxed poetic about the beauty of food storage and not having to make eight trips to the grocery store to get through a week. And then there was Ann:

> I hate my pantry! I really do. It's so loaded and difficult to access, it's sometimes not worth it to try to find what I want. On the other hand, how could I manage without one? I keep salsa, mac-n-cheese, pasta, pasta sauce, olives, soups, flour, sugar, pancake mix, syrup, oils, vinegars, pickles, mustard, ketchup, mayo, clams, tuna, spices,

cereal, oatmeal, popcorn, cake mixes, Jell-O, Crisco, chips, canned fruits, jellies, refried beans, black beans, kidney beans, chili and taco mix, salad dressings, and most things nonperishable before opening. I keep coffee, rice, potatoes, lentils, raisins, and nuts in a cabinet under the counter. It works, but I really have to keep it organized or things go stale and get lost or pile up in front of the very narrow space in front of the doors to the pantry shelves. I blame Y2K for causing bad habits of hoarding food.

And it's not just Y2K that we have to blame. Tim Jones, a researcher at the University of Arizona's Contemporary Archaeology Project, has spent years digging through people's garbage to see how much food the average American family throws away. At a whopping 470 pounds a year, that doesn't take a toll just on our budgets—it takes a toll on our planet. Between the land that's used to grow that food and then the land that's used to dispose of it, the impact is hard to ignore.

Besides guilt buying ("I'll buy the veggies because I know I should, but when I get home from work I'm too tired to cook") and poor planning, the other major factor to food waste is the proliferation of warehouse stores that induce us to buy things in bulk we may not be able to use before they go bad. (Have you ever bought fruit at Costco? Then you know what I mean.)

Just because Costco sells olive oil in half-gallon tubs doesn't mean you should buy it there. It's not a bargain if your oil goes rancid. Buy in bulk the things you have room to store and that you'll go through quickly.

Organize Your Pantry

Organize your pantry according to types of foods so that you can find things easily.

- *Grains:* rice, pasta, beans, oatmeal. Seal these tightly to prevent infestations. Also, remember that while grains keep well for a long time, they do eventually go rancid, especially whole grains.

- *Root vegetables:* onions, potatoes, yams, and the like. Just make sure to use them promptly.
- *Oils and sauces:* olive oil, vegetable oil, Worcestershire sauce, vinegar, and so on. Many sauces require refrigeration, so read the labels first.
- *Baking supplies:* baking soda, baking powder, flour, sugar, chocolate chips, salt, cooking spray.
- *Canned goods.*
- *Prepared foods and snacks:* crackers, cookies, dried fruit, chips, and anything else you like for munching.

It is tons of fun to look through magazines to see beautifully designed pantries with all their slide-out drawers, hidden cabinets, and baskets to make your space look beautiful. I have tried the beauty route for my pantry. It doesn't work. I have to organize my pantry like a grocery store: everything lined up in a row, clearly labeled and clearly visible. Each of my shelves has a purpose and a place for what's there.

I sound like a super-organized woman gone label happy. I'm not. I struggle to keep on top of my pantry. It's not the place I want to spend time getting creative. Here are some simple guidelines to keeping your pantry organized:

YOU HEREBY HAVE PERMISSION TO GET RID
OF THE STUFF YOU DO NOT USE.

You should hold no guilt for getting rid of food that you're not going to eat. One option is to donate it (along with some of the food that you do eat regularly) to a food pantry. Here is my local food bank's general list of most needed items.

The Food Bank needs nutritious, nonperishable foods:

- Meals in a can (stew, chili, soup)
- Tuna and canned meat
- Peanut butter
- Canned foods with pop-top lids

- Low-sugar cereals
- Canned fruit packed in juice
- Canned vegetables (low salt)

The Food Bank also needs nutritious, nonperishable, single-serving foods for use in programs for children:

- Pop-top tuna
- 100 percent fruit rolls
- Raisins
- Graham crackers
- Unsweetened applesauce
- Cheese and crackers
- Fruit cups
- Low-sugar cereal bowls
- Pretzels
- 100-percent fruit juice boxes
- Granola bars (without peanuts)

They ask that you not donate items packaged in glass or bulk quantities of rice, flour, and sugar. They do not have the resources to repackage and distribute those items.

So when you want to donate those unopened cans of sardines your dad left during Thanksgiving, be sure to toss in some canned peaches as well. Oh, and if you find any money stashed in your pantry, they will gladly accept that as well.

HERE'S ANOTHER CREATIVE WAY TO KEEP YOUR
PANTRY FROM GROWING OUT OF CONTROL.

I was once part of a mother's group that asked each member to bring in the extras from their pantry so they could set up an emergency pantry for those moms whose families were in a financial bind. You may want to check out whether your church or community center has a similar emergency food pantry in need of donations.

And if you have something the food pantry can't use? Dump it. That jar of homemade pickled carrots is doing no one any good sitting on your shelf. Let's be honest, even if the grocery stores were closed for days, don't you have plenty of other food you would eat before being desperate enough to choke down those carrots?

So do you get rid of the garbage (put those carrots down the garbage disposal, recycle the glass jar) or do you keep the garbage in your pantry, blocking the view of the food you really use?

Don't put new and exciting stuff into your pantry in the first place.

If you are a creative cook, this is going to be a hard one for you. Here are a couple of rules I have to live by when it comes to my pantry:

- Never "try something out to see if the family will like it" in a bulk size.

- Stock up only on things you have proven you will use up.

- If you are going to switch brands of something, try the smallest size available to see if the family likes it. That double-pack of cereal from the warehouse store is no bargain if no one will eat it. I have learned from experience that just because two cereal boxes both say "Raisin Bran," that doesn't mean my family thinks they're the same.

- Don't put items you use only rarely in your pantry. The pantry is for stocking up, not for red-and-green candy sprinkles. Either keep those in the kitchen, throw them away, or use them up on Valentine's and Saint Patrick's Day.

Keep a running list of pantry items to replenish.

Check out our downloadable list of some basic pantry items at www.ProjectsForYourSoul.com.

Having a well-stocked and well-organized pantry has been one of my key strategies to making mealtime less of a hassle. Pantry on, dudes!

Keeping a Pantry—The Freezer Version

I use my freezer as an extension of my pantry. This is where I stock up on everyday ingredients that need to stay frozen to last. I love this description that my friend Laura Joseph sent me of what she keeps stocked in her freezer for quick meals:

> Many days, I live out of my freezer. Here are some of the things I try to always have on hand:
>
> - *Frozen chicken tenders (not breaded).* They thaw much quicker and are a more appropriate portion size for kids and those of us who want to avoid going up a pant size. Also, they are great for stir-fries.
>
> - *A bag of precooked meatballs (usually turkey).* These are great for spaghetti and quick Swedish meatballs with noodles. Plus, in a pinch, you can throw almost any kind of sauce over those meatballs while heating them up in a saucepan, and have a quick appetizer or main dish (served over rice).
>
> - *Frozen salmon fillets.* One fillet can feed my family of four when I grill it and break it up over pasta.
>
> - *Precooked ground beef.* As soon as I get home from the warehouse store, I brown some ground beef with garlic and onions, let it cool, and then freeze it in gallon bags. It's easy to break up and you can use only the portion you need straight from the freezer.
>
> - *Frozen shrimp.* Great for a quick pasta dinner.

• • • • • • • • • • **Shrimp Alfredo** • • • • • • • • • • •

1 medium onion, chopped

2 cloves garlic, minced

1 T. butter

1 jar reduced-fat Alfredo sauce

¼ cup white wine

1 lb. frozen shrimp

12 oz. linguine, cooked and drained

2 T. minced fresh basil

In a medium saucepan, sauté onion and garlic in butter over a medium heat. Add Alfredo sauce and wine; simmer gently until heated through. Meanwhile, cook shrimp in boiling water just until shrimp turn pink, about 2 minutes. Drain. Spoon sauce over hot pasta; toss to coat well. Spoon shrimp over pasta. Serves 4–6.

• •

These are my basics. I also like to add pork chops and steak if I can get them at a good price and then freeze them in individual dinner sizes. A well-stocked freezer can sometimes last me three to four months.

Try This at Home

What's your next step to make your pantry more manageable?

- Find a place to put a pantry.
- Clean out the pantry you have.
- Put bulk purchases in large tubs.
- Make a list of things to keep your pantry stocked (or download our list at www.ProjectsForYourSoul.com).

Or as a Group

If you're serious about saving money and hassle by having a pantry, but you have no idea where you're going to store twenty-five pounds of flour, start your own food co-op with friends:

- I recommend no more than six people so it doesn't get too complicated.

- Figure out what items at least two of you use and would want to split.

- One of you hits the warehouse store with the compiled list of desired purchases.

- Once the shopper gets home, each member of the co-op comes over to pick up her purchases and pay her portion of the bill.

- If there are six people in the co-op and only four want flour, no problem. The flour gets divided into four parts, and each person who wanted flour pays a fourth of the cost.

- If you have freezer space, this works for freezer bulk purchases as well.

Part Three

GET YOUR FOOD

Chapter 9

Solution 5—Go to the Grocery Store Once a Week
(but get everything you need)

*"Ever consider what pets must think of us? I mean, here
we come back from a grocery store with the most
amazing haul—chicken, pork, half a cow.
They must think we're the greatest hunters on earth!"*

ANNE TYLER

Problem: I feel like I am at the grocery store every single
day of my life.

If there was one part of this whole process I could skip (or in my fantasies, have my own personal assistant manage) it would be the whole shopping thing. While making a list and checking it twice is nothing I'm ever going to love doing, I have found some ways to make the whole process manageable.

Take an Inventory

I do this about once a year, usually before a big cooking day. I go through the pantry, cupboards, freezer, and fridge and take stock of what I already have. This is also an excellent time to closely scrutinize all the expiration dates on my foods and use up the ones that are close to expiring and pitch the ones that are past their prime.

(*Warning:* My husband is deathly afraid that he's going to eat something that's one day past the date on the box. I can kind of understand that with milk, but dried pasta? This is one of those "Don't ask, don't tell" areas of our marriage. Use your own discretion, but if you have a spouse who has an especially itchy trigger finger—Roger will throw things away a month before their expiration date, "Just in case…"—beware.)

I have included inventory sheets on our website (www.Projects ForYourSoul.com) for you to download. Feel free to customize these inventory lists to fit your kitchen's needs. Just because I list something on the inventory sheets doesn't mean you need that item; these are just common grocery items for most families. There is also space for you to write in your family's specific favorites.

Here are the areas I want you to inventory:

- Freezer
- Refrigerator
- Pantry
- Cupboards
- Spices

Plan Backward

As I have mentioned in other parts of this book, one of the best strategies for cooking is to look at what you already have and plan your meals around those items. No sense buying chicken thighs for a recipe when you have a bunch of frozen drumsticks lurking in the back of the freezer. Besides, meat starts to lose its flavor or can suffer from freezer burn if it's on ice for months at a time.

So take a look at your list and see what you already have to cook with. Since meat is generally the most expensive part of the meal, use those items first. Then look through this book and your other favorite cookbooks to plan your meals around the ingredients you already have.

When looking for recipes, look for ones like those in this book that don't require a bunch of exotic ingredients and are simple to prepare. There's nothing worse than buying a tiny jar of poppy seeds for a "cheap" recipe only to discover that poppy seeds are anything but cheap. Use ingredients you are familiar with, and then allow yourself to experiment occasionally with one or two dishes that require a small number of unusual ingredients. If you don't like those ingredients, pitch them or give them to someone who will use them. There's no sense keeping a jar of chili paste you hated in your fridge door for a year if you're never going to use it again.

Check the Sales

Each Monday the sales flyers from my favorite grocery stores show up in my mailbox. I find out what the loss leaders are and see what meals I can create around those. If something is on a particularly good sale, I'll stock up if it will keep well, even if I'm not planning to use it right away. This is "shopping for my pantry," replenishing items that I like to have on hand or can get at a great price.

Make Your List

I shop a couple of different places, so I have a couple of different lists:

WAREHOUSE STORE—THIS IS WHERE
I DO MOST OF MY BULK SHOPPING:

- Frozen chicken breasts
- Whole roasted chickens
- Ground beef
- Pork roasts
- Pork chops
- Marinades
- Cheese
- Pasta
- Rice
- Canned veggies (especially tomatoes)
- Oatmeal
- Spices (only ones we use regularly)
- Vanilla (I use vanilla in mass quantities, and it is drastically cheaper at a warehouse store)
- Coffee
- Cereal
- Crackers
- Extra-virgin olive oil
- Butter
- Flour (since we bake a lot of our own breads)
- Popcorn
- Sugar for baking
- Honey

REGULAR GROCERY STORE:

- Produce (We stopped buying most produce at warehouse stores once we joined a veggie co-op. But when we want something specific, we buy it at the grocery store in order to get the quantity we need instead of the quantity we and our six neighbors would use if we bought it at a warehouse store.)
- Eggs
- Milk
- Meats I don't want to purchase in jumbo-packs (sausage, for example)
- Breads

Now let's be clear. Like you, I don't purchase all of these things every trip. And when we had more kids living at home, we bought eggs and milk at the warehouse store. But it's good to develop some guidelines for where you purchase what. We hit the warehouse store only about once a month these days, and since we have a tiny fridge, that dictates what we buy.

Try This at Home

If you are one of those super-organized people, many grocery stores offer a delivery service. We've done this a few times (once when we were going to be on vacation and needed groceries for the kids, and once when I was down with a bad back). I have a friend who has a standing order every week for milk, bread, bananas, and so on, and then just updates the order with whatever items she's running low on. She has small kids at home, so this is a lot better than having to manage three sets of grabby hands in the store.

Or as a Group

My friend Angela hates going to the warehouse store; she gets completely overwhelmed by the whole experience and the size of the packages. This has led to us sometimes going together or me picking up the items she needs. A side benefit is that we discovered we both purchase some of the same items (or discovered some items we both wanted to try) and get to split our loot.

I have found that Wednesday mornings at the warehouse store and one o'clock almost any weekday at the grocery store are great times to avoid the crowds.

Chapter 10

Solution 6—Other Places to Get Your Food

*"You don't have to cook fancy or complicated masterpieces—
just good food from fresh ingredients."*

JULIA CHILD

Problem: I'm just bored. We eat the same thing every single week. I hate thinking about cooking and it feels like just one more chore I have to do each day.

Part of the reason we resent the whole get-dinner-on-the-table process is that cooking can become drudgery if we're doing the same things over and over. As I was raising kids, I got mighty bored with the day in and day out of pasta and salads, casseroles and a side of veggies, and the same old same old that went on our plates. I was making dinner to get dinner on the table.

And that's OK. Sometimes.

But when you realize there are dozens of edible veggies on the planet and your family is in a rotation of about six, or when the only cheese you keep stocked in your house comes in individually wrapped slices, it may be time to get out of the grocery store and discover some new places to find your groceries. I want you to get inspired and start playing with your food.

Gardening

*"The act of putting into your mouth what the earth has grown
is perhaps your most direct interaction with the earth."*

FRANCES MOORE LAPPÉ

OK hear me out on this one.

Yes, I know that you're probably not going to save a ton of money through gardening.

And yes, I know it takes time to garden, and here we are trying to save time when it comes to meal preparation.

And yes, I know that most of us consider ourselves to have a black thumb.

I encourage you to try gardening anyway.

I know many of you are thinking, *How quaint. A garden. Perhaps she wants me to start milking my own grass-fed cows as well.*

I am a girl of the 'burbs. I have lived in townhomes and apartments most of my life. Most of my patios have been no bigger than a Yugo, but I have almost always had some sort of garden.

I would not consider myself your typical botany enthusiast. My mom has always had the ability to make things grow. (I remember the zucchini-on-steroids she grew when I was in second grade that my 6'4" dad used to complete his Jolly Green Giant costume for an office party at work.) But I have never had "the gift." I'm not good with which season is best for which plants, what the best varieties of tomatoes are, or even being a faithful waterer.

I have a lot of strikes against me.

However, I do have a garden. It may not impress those friends who love to discuss the pH of local soils, but it does provide my family with some great food, beautiful plants, and a whole lot of anticipation.

Advantages of Gardening

There are a bunch of advantages to having your own garden:

It's inspirational. Roger and I love to try new recipes and cooking techniques, and having a garden is just more inspiration. I will look up new recipes to try to use up some of our garden surplus.

It's educational. We started gardening while I was homeschooling, and the learning hasn't stopped. Not only did the kids learn about soil, sun, and water, I learn new things every year about how to grow better plants, make better food, and make a more comfortable home.

It's beautiful. I love a beautiful flower garden, but sometimes it can seem a little fussy to me. (Or maybe I'm just too lazy to grow anything without a delicious outcome.) There is just a special beauty to a vegetable garden. I love it when everything is in bloom and the bright red and orange of the tomatoes is popping against all that green. It's as if my whole back patio is dotted with little jewels.

It's delicious. If you've never eaten caprese salad (sliced tomatoes, basil, mozzarella cheese with herbs, oil, and vinegar) with veggies fresh off the vine, then you are missing one of the true pleasures of life.

For gardening, we keep it pretty simple. I used to blithely stroll down the aisle of Home Depot, throwing any interesting-looking plant into my basket. When I got home, I would dump the plant and some soil into a pot, put a saucer under it, and pray that something edible would come forth. But this lackadaisical approach was, not surprisingly, less than successful. Now I plant with a purpose.

After a lot of trial and error (and more than a few plants that gave their lives to my learning process), I have found some techniques that will give you a better chance of actually eating from your bounty.

Some Simple Tips to Make Your Garden Grow

KEEP IT REALLY SIMPLE.

To start with, I suggest you keep it simple with the plants you purchase. For the past several years we have planted a low-maintenance "salsa garden" and have enjoyed the variety and simplicity of that assortment every time. Here is what goes in our salsa garden:

- a variety of tomato plants
- peppers
- cilantro
- green onions

ASK AN EXPERT.

Explain to a garden-center employee that you want to start a garden but that you also want to keep it simple, and ask what you need. My own experience here is that it will do you no good to ask the seventeen-year-old at the giant home-supply store what are the best tomatoes to grow for an early harvest in your area. This is where the little mom-and-pop garden center shines. Ask one of the employees (who probably is growing her own garden at home) what you should get.

USE THE CORRECT CONTAINER.

Read those little tags carefully that tell you how big the pots you plant in should be or how far apart you should space your plants if they are going in the ground. I was crowding my plants and not getting the results I needed.

FIGURE OUT YOUR WATERING SYSTEM.

For most gardeners I know, they are their watering system. But since I travel a lot, it was important that I not rely on teenagers to keep my basil alive. If you don't want to rise at dawn every morning with a cup of coffee in one hand and a hose in the other, you may want to create an automated system, such as drip lines, for watering.

Creating a Kitchen Garden

I started to garden when I was homeschooling my kids back in the elementary grades. The house we owned had a small plot of dirt in a corner of the yard, just large enough for a few veggies. I have to say our first year was wildly unsuccessful. (Who knew that things like watering would be so essential?)

Fast forward several years. Roger and I decided to plant a salsa garden in containers on our back patio. We live in a townhouse, so my visions of sowing seed for major crops and my own henhouse have to be put on hold for a while.

We kept it simple the first year—just a few tomato plants, a couple of peppers, cilantro. But as our garden grew, so did our farmer-like confidence. This year, we planted more than a dozen tomato plants of every variety and size you could imagine. Our herb garden is abundant, and Roger has peppers aplenty to make all the mouth-burning recipes he can handle.

Here's what we have planted:

- a variety of tomato plants
- basil
- cilantro
- parsley
- a variety of hot and mild peppers

- green onions
- green garlic
- zucchini
- squash

We have learned a few things in the couple of years we've been playing around with amateur gardening:

It is not necessary to purchase every tomato plant available at Home Depot. Starting off with a half-dozen plants is a great place to begin.

Pick some early bloomers and some late bloomers. Otherwise, everything comes in at once and you go from famine to feast in a matter of days. (And, if you happen to be on vacation when all the tomatoes come in, it may be an indication to the worms of your neighborhood that you don't want your tomatoes and that you were kind enough to plant a smorgasbord just for them.)

Install a drip irrigation system. I am a stingy waterer. I always have better things to do (probably something involving a rerun of *The Office*) than stand in the backyard with a hose.

But as soon as Roger installed our drip system, I was *amazed* at what a difference watering makes. (Yeah, I know. Duh.) For less than $60, our entire backyard crop is downright lush because of the daily hit of water. If you embrace routine and love the meditative state of watering—great. Otherwise, get a drip system and get it on a timer. When you're sitting down to enjoy the season's first bruschetta topped with your homegrown tomatoes, you'll thank me.

Here is the recipe that inspired us to plant the garden in the first place. (I have included the canned-ingredient version as well for non-gardeners, or if you want to make salsa out of season.)

• • • • • • • • • • • **Roger's Salsa** • • • • • • • • • • • •
(Roger Lipp)

12 tomatoes (or two large cans of crushed tomatoes)

1 15-oz. can of tomato sauce

1 bunch cilantro, chopped coarse down to the stemmy part

2 stems green onion, chopped medium

2 slices red onion, chopped medium (I use slices from the center portion)

2 jalapeños, chopped fine (leave seeds in)—if you want mild salsa, substitute Anaheim peppers; if you want hot salsa, substitute 4 habaneros

4-5 garlic cloves, chopped fine

Combine these ingredients in a large glass bowl. If tomatoes were room temperature to start with, add two ice cubes and stir. Add the following seasonings to taste (measurements given are approximate):

2 T. fresh oregano leaves, chopped

1 T. cumin powder

1 T. coarse-ground black pepper

1 T. fresh basil, chopped

1 tsp. marjoram

• •

I have to admit I was pretty jealous of Roger and his world-famous (OK, maybe more friend- and family-famous) salsa, but now I have bragging rights of my own—bruschetta.

I spent weeks working on a recipe—finding what other people were doing, tweaking and tweaking until I got something that I loved. Now when I'm asked to bring something to a party, I make the bruschetta several hours ahead and let it set in the fridge so all the flavors meld.

● ● ● ● ● ● ● ● ● ● ● ● **Bruschetta** ● ● ● ● ● ● ● ● ● ● ● ●
(Kathi Lipp)

⅓ cup olive oil

3 tsp. balsamic vinegar

⅛ cup chopped fresh basil or 1/2 tsp. dried

Pinch of freshly ground black pepper

4-5 medium, ripe tomatoes (I prefer Roma, but any firm tomato will do) seeded and chopped. Drain in a strainer for 15 minutes. (You can use a paper or cloth towel to very gently press out the extra moisture)

2 baguettes, cut into ½-inch slices

4 cloves garlic, sliced in half

½ cup grated Parmesan cheese

Combine oil, vinegar, basil, and pepper in a large bowl and whisk together. Add drained tomatoes to oil and vinegar and toss to coat. Allow to marinate for at least 15 minutes and up to 4 hours.

Toast bread slices on one side, flip, and then sprinkle with Parmesan cheese on the other. Once toasted, rub the cut side of the garlic on the top of each slice. Top each slice with the tomato mixture. Serves 8 as an appetizer.

● ●

Nothing makes me feel more "gardeny" than to go out to our back patio and harvest dinner. The recipe below is a pretty simple dish, but nothing will highlight your gardening prowess better.

Garden Pasta

8 Roma tomatoes, seeded and diced

2 cloves of garlic, minced

½ cup butter, melted

¼ cup chopped fresh basil (or 1 T. dried)

8 oz. dried angel hair pasta, cooked

¼ cup Parmesan cheese, grated (or to taste)

Combine tomatoes and garlic in a saucepan. Simmer for 15 minutes, then set aside. Toss pasta with butter and basil. Stir in tomatoes and serve with Parmesan cheese grated on top. Serves 6.

If I could have only one item growing in my garden, it would be tomatoes. If I could have only two, the second item would be bushels and bushels of basil. Make this pesto one time and you'll want to install an indoor hothouse to grow basil year-round.

Garden Pesto

2 cups fresh basil leaves

4 tsp. minced garlic

2 T. pine nuts, roasted

⅓ cup extra-virgin olive oil

2 T. fresh-grated Parmesan

Salt and pepper, to taste

Chop the basil, garlic, and pine nuts in a food processor. With the motor running, drizzle in the oil. Blend in the cheese, salt, and pepper.

Farmers' Markets

"If junk food is the devil, then a sweet orange is as scripture."

AUDREY FORIS

I love just-picked produce, homemade breads, strawberries the size of a baby's fist. And if you're like me, you spend a lot of time at your local farmers' market. I couldn't agree more with author Allison Bottke and her ode to farmers' markets:

> The farmers' market in Faribault, MN, was my "home away from home" many a Saturday morning for almost 15 years. After moving to Texas in 2008, I was happy to discover a farmers' market beginning in the nearby town of Keller, TX. It's not just fresh produce and handmade crafts, but the opportunity to meet the people responsible for bringing these things to us. It's about building relationships and getting back to the basics of what made our country strong in the first place.

I love several things about our local farmers' market:

Getting to buy locally. I love knowing that the dollars I'm using to purchase my asparagus are going into the pockets of people in my community (some of them even friends). I also love knowing that the tax on these purchases is going to pave the roads I use and build the parks my kids have played in.

Getting to know the growers. I love knowing the history behind the farms that are growing my food. What is it that keeps these growers committed to this lifestyle? How did they decide on the crops they grow? Being an amateur gardener, I'm becoming a veggie nerd and love to know all the inside dirt.

The taste. I may not be able to tell the difference between all grocery-store veggies and fruits and the ones at the market, but tomatoes? Don't try to pass a store-bought one across my table. I'm like a drug-sniffing dog when it comes to anything going into my homemade pasta sauce.

The inspiration. I go to the grocery store to feed my troops. I go to the farmers' market to create meals. I love going with one of my favorite market meals in mind and getting the best ingredients to make it really special.

Do Your Research

Check out your farmers' market on the web before you hit it. Lots of websites will point you to various markets around the country, but I find their information to be sometimes out-of-date, or some of my favorite markets are left off completely. My best hint is to just do a web search with your zip code or town name and the words "farmers market."

On the market's website, you'll get an idea of the type of vendors who show up, the hours of operation, as well as other important information. (Are animals allowed at the market? Are they open when it's raining? What is the start date, and when do they close?)

Know Your Seasons and Regions

It's not lost on me that when I go to visit our family in Georgia, the strawberries my niece serves me are from Watsonville, California, about thirty miles west of where I live. Yep, the strawberries traveled farther than I did.

If you know which foods are likely to be available when you get to your farmers' market, making decisions at each stall is much easier. Learn what grows in your area when and talk to the growers about what will be coming to market in upcoming weeks.

I asked some of my farmers' market friends around the country what they find when they shop the stalls.

The Southwest (Carol Boley)

"Living here in Phoenix (the Garden Spot of America!), the farmers' markets offer not only the expected wide variety of organic and pesticide-free produce, but also cheeses, jams, tamales, fresh salsas, and sometimes shrimp caught off the coast of Mexico. Seasonal specialties include apples and cider from Arizona orchards. Crafts and fresh flowers are popular also. As an aside, the best tomatoes I ever ate were from a farmer's stand in Maryland outside Washington, DC. When I asked the farmer where he grew them, he said they came off a truck that brought them from California. Apparently the driver bypasses Arizona en route to Maryland, because I have never been able to find such delicious tomatoes in my state. I learned to always ask where the produce is grown!"

The Atlantic Coast/Florida (Angela Hood)

"I live in Central Florida, and our local farmers' market runs almost all year long; they only take off the winter from roughly November to February. We also have a couple of permanent fruit stands in town that are year-round. Of course, being in Florida, oranges are always a good choice. My personal favorite for May and June is watermelon. During the summer months, I love to grab some sugar snap peas for a snack. My three-year-old daughter and I like to eat them fresh out of the bag. Tomatoes are always a big hit in the summer. Blueberries are ripe for the picking at local farms in March. Strawberries are very popular in February; we even have a festival about thirty miles south of us. Corn is a hot commodity in May and June—sweet corn, white corn, yellow corn. And I've grown tomatoes and potatoes with great success."

The Midwest (Dawn Arbogast)

"I lived in Iowa most of my life. Usually farmers' markets start in May, but it isn't worth going until the summer. Compared to California (where I now live), Iowa has much less fruit. Some popular veggies are green beans, asparagus, peas, and especially sweet corn. My favorite corn was a yellow-and-white variety called peaches and cream. In late summer, people sell melons and muskmelon (cantaloupe). In the fall there are lots of apples. In our family garden we also grew onions, beets, and radishes."

The West (Sarah Read)

"We have a few farmers' markets in the Salt Lake City area, but the one I like best is the Downtown Farmers' Market open mid-June to mid-October. The kids and I are always on the lookout for fruits and veggies that we cannot get at the small farm stands near our house. We always buy berries there—raspberries, blueberries, and blackberries. Apricots and peaches when they ripen (July). Melons are available all summer. Plenty of squashes, sugar snap peas, and heirloom tomatoes. Sadly, we never have strawberries. Onions and potatoes are later in the fall, and the pumpkin festival is on the last Saturday they are open in October. The kids love it, and we always get extra."

Texas (Karen Porter)

"I live near Houston and the Gulf Coast, and we have warm weather early (around March or April). Planting starts early, and we have fresh produce by May or June. The farmers' market I go to began in 1934 when a local farmer and his wife sold veggies on the side of the road. Now the grandson runs the massive farm and a huge pavilion is open every day (except Christmas). The grandmother still comes to the pavilion every day and sits in a big white rocker and talks to all who come. The spring season begins in March when we can go into the strawberry fields and pick juicy red berries. We make it a family outing. The biggest thrill of the season is early June when the first tomatoes are ready. First we get big green tomatoes to fry up southern style. Then later we buy vine-ripened red tomatoes that taste like candy."

Be Prepared

The Boy Scouts had the right idea. Spend a little time preparing before you go to your farmers' market and you'll have an easier time getting meals on the table. Here are a few things I recommend in advance of shopping the stalls:

- Bring a small cooler packed with ice.
- Bring plenty of shopping bags (both plastic and cloth).
- Have a wad of ones and fives as well as some quarters. It's great if you don't have to wait for change at every stall.
- Wear comfortable shoes and clothes.

- Put on sunscreen before you leave.
- Carry pen and paper to write down the names of new veggies you buy. That way you can search through your recipe books and on the web for ways to use the new treasure. Sometimes I write down the website of a particular vendor for a recipe or to order something from them. (This beats having to bust open a blueberry to write stuff on my arm.)

Go in With a (Meal) Plan

If you know what's in season you can easily make a meal plan to bring with you. Yes, it will help remind you of all the things you need, but more importantly, it will keep you from buying a bunch of things you don't need that will just end up going bad in the fridge.

When I'm at the farmers' market, I get very optimistic about the amount of fruit and veggies my family will eat. If I don't go in with a list, I will buy enough asparagus to cater a formal sit-down dinner for a dozen.

So come in with a plan for the week's dinners, but be willing to be flexible. If the veggies are particularly tempting, you have my blessing to scrap the frozen lasagna on Thursday and replace it with an Asian stir-fry.

Pick Up One Surprise Every Trip

Yes, you should make a plan and stick to it, but part of the fun of farmers' markets is using fresh new-to-you ingredients in your cooking. Every single trip I pick up one new item—we've tried everything from kohlrabi (German turnips) and rapini (broccoli rabe) to flourless, sugarless cookies (that actually *rocked*). We have found several new favorites by trying veggies that looked as if they grew on an entirely different planet.

Take in the Whole Experience

When a farmer cuts up an Asian pear for you to try, don't refuse. That man is like Picasso with a paintbrush—he is proud of the fruit of his labors (sorry, couldn't resist) and wants to share it with an appreciative audience.

When the vendor isn't busy, ask for suggestions on how to prepare new foods, or ask for recommendations about what you should be purchasing right now.

Go Early or Go Late

Go early for the best selection. Go late to get deals as these farmers don't want to carry anything home. I have seen fruit prices slashed in half at the end of the day.

Have Cart, Will Buy

When I saw my mother-in-law's wire shopping cart, I became downright green with envy. I knew I had to own one specifically for all the green purchases I make at the farmers' market.

If you frequent farmers' markets, you'll be grateful to have a fold-up cart in which to collect—and protect—all your purchases. And make sure it's collapsible; you still need to fit it into your car along with the six flats of strawberries.

If your market is crowded or the aisles are too narrow for a cart, bring a backpack and a lot of cloth shopping bags.

Buy Yourself a Prize

Hey, you've been working hard to provide variety and yumminess for your family—treat yourself to some farmers' market flowers to put in your kitchen or on the dinner table. The prettier your kitchen, the easier it is to spend time in there making great meals.

When You Get Home

You will thank yourself if you get everything washed and bagged when you get home. I get out my salad spinner and wash up the greens, rinse all the fruits and veggies (except ones that shouldn't be washed until they are ready to be eaten, such as strawberries), and make up a few dishes while the inspiration is rife.

Here is one of my favorite all-purpose fruit recipes. I often make this when I get my new batch of fruit:

● ● ● ● ● ● ● **Pick Your Fruit Oatmeal Crisp** ● ● ● ● ● ● ●

½ cup firmly packed brown sugar, divided in half

2 T. flour

¾ tsp. cinnamon, divided into ½ and ¼ tsps.

6 cups peeled, seeded, and sliced apples, pears,
  or peaches

¼ cup water

¼ cup butter, softened

1 cup old-fashioned oats, uncooked

Preheat oven to 350°. Lightly grease 8-inch glass pan. Combine ¼ cup brown sugar, flour, and ½ tsp. cinnamon. Stir in fruit and water. Set aside. Combine oats, ¼ cup brown sugar, butter, and ¼ tsp. cinnamon. Spoon fruit into baking dish. Top with oat mixture. Bake for 40 to 45 minutes or until fruit is tender.

● ●

● ● ● ● ● ● ● ● ● ● ● ● **Zucchini Dip** ● ● ● ● ● ● ● ● ● ● ●

1 zucchini

1 cup plain low-fat yogurt

1 clove of garlic, minced

In your food processor, shred enough zucchini for ½ cup Put the zucchini in a colander and press out all the excess moisture with a paper towel. Put the zucchini in a medium bowl and mix with yogurt and garlic. Chill for one hour and serve with fresh market veggies. (Sometimes I'll add a dash of dill, Italian seasonings, or curry powder to taste.)

● ●

And this has to be the ultimate farmers' market recipe:

• • • • • • • • • • • • **Ratatouille** • • • • • • • • • • • •

1 onion, diced

2-3 garlic cloves, pressed

1 T. olive oil

4-5 zucchini, cubed

1 large eggplant, peeled and cubed

2-3 lb. fresh tomatoes or 2 cans whole peeled tomatoes, drained

¼ lb. mushrooms

½ tsp. each oregano, basil, garlic salt, salt, parsley, Italian herb mix

1 cup shredded cheese

Sauté onion and garlic in oil. Add zucchini, eggplant, tomatoes, and mushrooms. Cover and simmer at least ½ hour and up to 2 hours. Add spices and simmer 10 minutes to 1 hour. Drain off the juices and transfer to a casserole dish. Cover with grated cheese and bake at 350° for 15 minutes or until cheese melts.

• •

Try This at Home

If this is your first attempt at gardening, spend some time with a gardening nerd at your local garden center and ask for recommendations of plants that grow well in your area (tomatoes and basil can be grown pretty much anywhere but the most extreme climates). Start with one or two plants to get the hang of it.

Or as a Group

Does someone in your group have a green thumb? How about having a gardening day? No book could ever cover what would grow best in your backyard, but I'm sure someone in your group would love to share their local knowledge.

I love what Jennifer Beauchamp of Tucson, Arizona, does to celebrate the growing season. One of her friends will open up her house and throw a "Dirt Party." You see, Jennifer is from farm folk and has never met a bag of steer manure she didn't like. But now that she lives in the very dry city that is Tucson, several of her friends (and their friends) are desperate for her country knowledge on how to keep their plants from dying.

Every guest brings a plant that needs to be repotted. The men do the hauling (manure, potting soil, dirt), and the women get their hands dirty repotting the plants in Jennifer's special mix: one-third local soil, one-third potting soil, and one-third steer manure. Everyone swears by Jennifer's not-so-secret formula, and all the plant owners go home with healthier plants.

If you know a person with a green thumb, you may want to throw your own "Dirt Party" and get your hands dirty in spring for salsa in the summer.

Part Four

GET COOKING

Chapter 11

Freezer Cooking

"Hey baby, do you like fine cooking? Cause you know what?
I got Swanson's Dinner in the freezer with your name on it."
JIMMY FALLON

The Problem: I hate having to cook on the busiest nights of the week. I wish dinner were just waiting at home for me.

It all started innocently enough. My husband was working long days as an engineer with an even longer commute. I was busy with our two small kids and running a business from the office (read *playroom*) of our tiny home. After a day of dishes, diapers, and purchase orders, dinner was the last thing on my mind. Unfortunately, it was not the last thing on my family's mind.

So, like so many moms before me, I would resort to takeout food, breakfast cereal, and resentment. Why am I the only one around here who has to think about dinner? Everyone in this house has two arms. (It didn't occur to me at the time that two of those people were under the age of four, and the other was out of the house for eleven hours a day.)

Kathi v. Freezer Cooking

Enter *Once-a-Month Cooking* by Mimi Wilson and Mary Beth Lagerborg. This little book showed women like me how they could cook for a day and eat for a month by preparing thirty different meals for the freezer. This book revolutionized my life.

Suddenly, I was the freezer queen. I was shopping and cooking, chopping and freezing. It gave me such satisfaction to stand back and look at the thirty meals snug in the freezer, waiting to be served to friends and family. It was so comforting to know what was for dinner each night. Our cereal consumption went way down.

However, after a while, my family started to tire of the same recipes, month after month. I was an inexperienced cook, and trying to get other recipes to work for the freezer system seemed like too big a job.

Reunited—Back to the Freezer

Fast-forward a few years. My kids are both in school during the day, and I work those same hours out of the house. I harkened back to the days of dinners waiting to be popped in the oven as soon as I walked through the door instead of the four o'clock mad dash to the grocery store I was currently making. I knew I had to get back into the freezer-meal game.

This time, however, I had a new tool at my disposal: the Internet. I did a Google search and came up with more recipes for freezer meals than I could cook in a lifetime. Then I started to talk with other friends who were experimenting with freezer cooking. Suddenly, I was swapping recipes with friends both online and next door. I started to prepare a few meals, freeze them, and serve them to my family and friends. There were more hits than misses, and I knew I could fit freezer cooking back into our busy lives.

You Could Be a Freezer Cooker if...

Are you wondering if freezer cooking is for you? Here are some reasons that I love to freezer cook:

- It reduces my stress by having meals ready to go every night.
- It reduces my shopping bill by letting me shop for inexpensive ingredients and on-sale meat.
- It helps me help others. I am always able to deliver a meal to someone who just had a baby, has a sick family member, or is in a financial crunch.
- It lets me customize meals for special diets.

Freezer-Cooking Guidelines

On the next few pages, I will give you some guidelines for freezer cooking, as well as some recipes that have proven to be crowd pleasers for dozens of my friends and family. But first a warning: freezer cooking can become an addiction. I get a high off having dozens of meals stocked in my freezer, waiting to be put to use in our home or the homes of people we love. Once you try it, you might decide that your freezer is your favorite appliance in the kitchen.

Provisions: Shopping for the Big Day

Once you decide on your recipes, it's time to put together a shopping list. When you triple recipes (which I recommend if you're doing bulk freezer cooking), it's much easier and cheaper to buy in bulk. If you're creating similar recipes (all-Italian, all-Mexican), you might be able to buy your sauces and seasonings in bulk as well. If you have leftover chicken breasts or ground beef after preparing your meals, you can pour extra marinade over the chicken breasts and freeze, or turn the ground beef into taco meat with taco seasonings and some chopped onions.

Before shopping, it's a good idea to clean out your freezer and refrigerator to make room for all the food you're bringing home from the store. It also enables you to figure out for sure what you already have that you can use for your big cooking day.

Production: Cooking on the Big Day

As mentioned before, you'll want to spend some time preparing your ingredients. I often do this as soon as I get home and leave the actual cooking for the next day. Here are some of the tasks you can do in advance of your big cooking day:

- Brown ground beef
- Cook chicken for casseroles
- Chop veggies (can be stored in the refrigerator in a little cold water)

- Cook rice and pasta (pasta can be stored in a plastic bag with a little bit of vegetable oil so it doesn't stick to the bag)
- Prepare some of the marinades and place them in gallon bags

Everything you do on prep day will make it that much easier on cooking day.

C-Day (Cooking Day)

Make sure you have a good breakfast and wear comfortable shoes. Put on some fun music that makes you want to dance. You'll need that energy for cooking.

- Tackle one recipe at a time. If I try to do too many recipes at once, I get confused and sometimes end up with chicken cacciatore with a slightly Mexican flair. My family can be so unadventurous sometimes.
- Clean as you go—you'll be glad you did at the end of the day.
- Double bag all the marinades to avoid any unfortunate accidents.
- When freezing casseroles, wrap the pan in foil and bag the casseroles in a freezer bag.
- As you bag up your dinners, use your permanent marker to label each with the name of the dish, reheating instructions, and the date it was assembled.

What Not to Freeze
- Cake icing made with egg whites
- Cream filling and soft frostings
- Pies made with custard or cream fillings
- Cooked egg whites
- Fried foods

- Fruit jelly
- Soft cheese (unless mixed into a recipe)
- Mayonnaise (unless mixed into a recipe)
- Sour cream (unless mixed into a recipe)
- Potatoes

Freezer Safety

- Thaw foods in the refrigerator overnight, or if in a freezer bag, defrost in the microwave. Never thaw foods at room temperature.

- Do not cook food in freezer bags in the microwave.

- Any food that looks or smells suspect—toss! Food experts suggest that you keep your meals no more than three months in the freezer.

How to Freeze Prepared Meals

Freezing your food falls into two different categories: (1) casseroles, and (2) soups, stews, chili, and marinades. Here's how to freeze each category:

CASSEROLES

For casserole freezing, I have used disposable 8 x 8 foil cake pans (available at places like Target and Walmart) for years.

My addiction to foil cake pans started when I was doing our freezer-cooking swap with a bunch of other girls (directions on how to start your own group are coming up). We would each make our dinners at home, and then bring them to a predetermined location and swap. We didn't want the hassle of returning dishes, so the cake pans worked great.

But it was a little silly when cooking a casserole to freeze for my own family to still use the foil pans. Besides the cost, it wasn't the most environmentally wise solution. So I finally broke down and bought a dozen of those inexpensive (OK, cheap) steel pans from Target.

Here are my instructions for packaging the casseroles in either a steel, glass, or foil pan:

1. Spray the bottom of the serving pan with nonfat cooking spray.

2. Put your casserole in the pan.

3. Cover the casserole with foil.

4. Label the foil with the name and date of the casserole.

5. Slip the 8 x 8 pan into a gallon-sized Ziploc bag with the printing on the bag facing down.

OK, here's the money/environmental tip of the day: If you label the foil instead of the bag (which is just keeping your food from freezer burn and isn't touching any food), you can reuse your Ziploc bag to protect other meals. If you bag your food with a label on the foil and put the Ziploc imprint on the bottom of the casserole, you'll be able to see clearly what is in your pan. Those baggies are expensive, and it's my goal to make them last as long as possible.

If you don't have all the pans you need, here's a great suggestion from one of my blog readers, Deanna: "To save more money I suggest lining a casserole dish with aluminum foil and then preparing the meal in it. Freeze it, lift the meal out of the casserole dish, wrap the meal in another layer of foil, label it, and stick it back in the freezer. When you go to cook it, just unwrap the outer layer of foil, pop the meal back in the original dish, and cook. Makes clean up a breeze too!"

Soups, Stews, Chili, and Marinades

Freezing this food category is just as easy, maybe a little bit easier, than freezing casseroles:

1. Label a gallon bag with the name of the meal and the date it was prepared.

2. Put your meal in the gallon bag. You can use a cleaned out coffee can (or your husband) to hold up the baggie while you ladle in the soup or stew or marinade.

3. Seal up the baggie most of the way, leaving a small opening to squeeze out all the excess air to help prevent freezer burn.

4. Seal the first baggie up in another baggie (again, to avoid freezer burn).

5. Place a cookie sheet in your freezer and lay your meal on the cookie sheet. This not only will keep your meal from freezing through the slats of your freezer (thereby ensuring you don't get to eat that meal until the next time you defrost), but it also makes that meal as compact as possible, allowing you to stack more meals in a tight space.

Here are some of our family's and friends' favorite recipes. Why are they favorites? Because a majority of the kids would actually eat them!

• • • • • • • • • • • • **Baked Ziti** • • • • • • • • • • • • •

(My kids love this recipe. They even eat their veggies without complaining when we serve it.)

1 lb. ground beef

¼ chopped onion

16 oz. penne pasta, parboiled and drained

6 cups spaghetti sauce

6 slices mozzarella cheese

½ cup Parmesan cheese

Prepare: Brown ground beef and onions together. Add spaghetti sauce. Combine sauce and cooked pasta; mix well.

Freeze: Spread pasta in 9 x 13 pan and cover with foil. Attach two freezer bags to pan, one with the mozzarella cheese slices, one with grated Parmesan cheese. Freeze.

Serve: Thaw casserole and cheeses. Place mozzarella cheese slices over casserole. Sprinkle Parmesan cheese over casserole. Cover and bake at 350° for 30 minutes or until the cheese is bubbly. Remove the foil and bake for 5 more minutes. Serves 4.

• •

• • • • • • • • • Chicken and Chips • • • • • • • • • •

3 cups diced, cooked chicken

1 can cream of chicken soup

½ cup sour cream

¼ cup salsa

2 cups shredded Monterey Jack cheese

2 cups crushed corn chips

Prepare: Combine chicken, soup, sour cream, and salsa. Spoon half of this mixture into casserole dish. Top with half the cheese and 1 cup of the crushed corn chips. Repeat.

Freeze: Cover with foil and freeze.

Serve: Defrost overnight and reheat in a 350° oven for 35 minutes. Serves 4.

• • • • • • • • • • Chicken Burritos • • • • • • • • • •

1¼ cups rice

1 14-oz. can refried beans

2 cups Monterey Jack cheese

2 cups boneless, skinless chicken breasts

1 20-oz. can green enchilada sauce

6 tortillas

Prepare: Cook the rice according to package directions. Grate the cheese. Cook and shred the chicken breasts.

Assemble: Spread each tortilla with refried beans. Mix the shredded chicken with half the enchilada sauce. Spoon the chicken mixture and rice into the tortillas. Sprinkle with half the cheese. Roll and place seam-side down in a 8 x 8 pan covered with ¼ cup enchilada sauce. Cover with remaining sauce and cheese.

Freeze: Wrap in foil and freeze.

Serve: Defrost in refrigerator overnight. Bake at 350° for 30 minutes with foil removed. Serves 4.

(If we're having guests, I'll pick up a taco salad kit, chips and salsa, and limes to squeeze over the salad.)

• •

• • • • • • • • • • **Chicken Cacciatore** • • • • • • • • • •

1 lb. boneless, skinless chicken breasts

1 T. vegetable oil

1¼ cups onion

2 cups mushrooms

1 tsp. minced garlic

1 28-oz. can crushed tomatoes in puree

2 T. parsley

¼ tsp. pepper

2 tsp. Italian seasoning

1 tsp. basil

Parmesan cheese

Prepare: Cut chicken into cubes. Slice onions and mushrooms. Chop garlic.

Cook: In a large skillet, sauté chicken in vegetable oil until no longer pink in the center. Remove chicken from skillet and sauté onions, mushrooms, and garlic until the onions are transparent. Add chicken and remaining ingredients except for Parmesan cheese. Simmer for 15 minutes. Allow sauce to cool.

Freeze: Freeze in a 13x9 pan.

Serve: Thaw sauce in the refrigerator overnight. Place the foil-covered pan in a 350° oven for 30 minutes to warm. Serve over pasta or mashed potatoes. Serves 4.

(I like to serve this with a crisp tossed salad and rosemary bread.)

• •

● ● ● ● ● ● ● ● ● ● **Chicken Manicotti** ● ● ● ● ● ● ● ● ● ●

(So rich, so wonderful. This is a once-every-three-months treat for our family.)

1 T. butter, melted

3 cups cooked chicken breasts, shredded

2 cups low-fat ricotta cheese

½ cup mozzarella or Parmesan cheese

1 tsp. dried parsley

2 eggs, lightly beaten

4 cups tomato sauce

14 manicotti shells, parboiled, still firm

Prepare: In a large skillet, brown chicken in butter or margarine for 3 minutes. Mix chicken, both cheeses, spices, and eggs. Cover the bottom of your pan with tomato sauce. Stuff the manicotti shells with the chicken mixture and place in pan, sides touching. Cover with remaining sauce.

Freeze: Cover pans with foil and freeze.

Serve: Thaw. Sprinkle manicotti with Parmesan or mozzarella cheese. Bake uncovered at 350° for 30 minutes. Serves 6.

● ●

● ● ● ● ● ● ● ● ● ● **Dreamy Spaghetti** ● ● ● ● ● ● ● ● ● ●

8 oz. spaghetti

15 oz. tomato sauce

8 oz. cream cheese

1 lb. ground beef

½ lb. cottage cheese

¼ cup sour cream

⅓ cup green onion, minced

Parmesan cheese

Prepare: Cook spaghetti and drain. Brown ground beef and drain. Combine spaghetti, ground beef, tomato sauce, and season to taste. Remove from heat. Combine cheeses, sour cream, and onion in another dish. In casserole or 8 x 8 foil pan, spread one-half of the spaghetti; cover with cheese mixture. Cover with remaining spaghetti. Spread tomato sauce mixture over all.

Freeze: Cover pan with aluminum foil (spray foil with cooking oil so that acid from tomato sauce doesn't touch the foil).

Serve: Sprinkle Parmesan cheese on top. Bake at 350° for 45 minutes. Serves 4.

• •

Freezer Meatballs

2 lb. lean ground beef

1 cup dry, unseasoned bread crumbs

2 eggs

1½ tsp. salt

¼ tsp. pepper

Prepare: Mix all ingredients. Divide mixture into 32 equal portions and roll into meatballs.

Freeze: Place in freezer on tray until frozen; pack into two one-gallon bags.

Serve: Cook meatballs in a medium skillet until they are no longer pink in the middle. Serves 8.

• •

• • • • • • • • • Green-Chile Enchiladas • • • • • • • • • • •

(Mexican food in minutes—*yum!*)

5 tortillas

3 cups chicken breasts, chopped

3 green onions, finely diced

1 small can diced green chilies

½ lb. Monterey Jack cheese, shredded, divided

1 large can green-chili enchilada sauce

Prepare: Pour a small amount of enchilada sauce to cover bottom of square baking dish. Combine chicken, chilies, onions, and cheese, leaving a small amount of cheese for the top of the enchiladas. Place an equal amount of chicken mixture into each tortilla and roll. Pour remaining sauce on top of enchiladas and top with remaining cheese.

Freeze: Cover pan with foil and freeze.

Serve: Defrost in the refrigerator overnight. Bake at 350° for 40 minutes or until bubbly. Serves 4.

• • • • • • • • • • Grilled Flank Steak • • • • • • • • • • •

1 cup soy sauce

½ cup brown sugar

½ cup unsweetened pineapple juice

½ cup Italian salad dressing

½ cup red wine vinegar

½ cup Worcestershire sauce

1 tsp. salt

1 clove garlic

1½ lb. flank steak

Prepare: Mix all the above ingredients and pour over the flank steak in a gallon bag.

Freeze: Double bag the flank steak. Freeze lying down.

Serve: Defrost in refrigerator overnight. Grill steak over hot charcoal for 5 to 10 minutes on each side. Slice thinly across the grain. Serves 4.

• •

• • • • • • • • • Hillary's Teriyaki Chicken • • • • • • • • • •

2 cups teriyaki sauce

1 cup water

8 cloves garlic, minced

2 tsp. ginger, ground

4 boneless, skinless chicken breasts

Prepare: Mix all the ingredients together. Pour over chicken breasts in a one-gallon bag.

Freeze: Double bag the chicken. Freeze lying flat.

Serve: Thaw chicken overnight in the refrigerator. Drain marinade. Place chicken breasts in a pan sprayed with light cooking oil. Bake at 350° for 30 to 40 minutes. Serves 4.

• •

• • • • • • • • • Honey-Mustard Chicken • • • • • • • • • •

1 stick butter, melted

¼ cup Dijon mustard

½ cup honey

4-6 boneless, skinless chicken breasts

Prepare: Mix all the ingredients together. Pour over chicken breasts in a one-gallon bag.

Freeze: Double bag the chicken. Freeze lying flat.

Serve: Thaw chicken overnight in the refrigerator. Drain marinade. Place chicken breasts in a pan sprayed with light cooking oil. Bake at 350° for 30 to 40 minutes. Serves 4.

• •

● ● ● ● ● ● ● ● ● ● **Jalapeño Flank Steak** ● ● ● ● ● ● ● ● ● ● ●

6 jalapeños

8 cloves garlic

1 T. cracked black pepper

2 T. coarse salt

½ cup lime juice

2 T. dried oregano

1 cup olive oil

1½ lb. flank steak

Prepare: Combine all ingredients except steak in blender and puree. Pour over steak and rub in. Marinate in refrigerator for 2 to 24 hours or freeze for later use.

Freeze: Double bag and freeze.

Serve: Grill steak on the barbecue or cut it up and stir-fry for fajita meat. Serves 4.

Note: You can double this recipe and heat marinade on stove to have extra sauce to pour over steak.

● ●

● ● ● ● ● ● ● ● ● ● **Kathy's Pork Chops** ● ● ● ● ● ● ● ● ● ● ●

(Sounds weird when you read the ingredients, but it's wonderful!)

4 boneless pork chops

1 packet onion soup mix

1½ cups Thousand Island dressing

1½ cups apricot preserves (not jelly)

Prepare: Mix all ingredients except pork chops together. Pour over pork chops in a one-gallon bag.

Freeze: Double bag the pork chops. Freeze lying flat.

Serve: Thaw pork chops overnight in the refrigerator. Drain marinade. Place pork chops in a pan sprayed with light cooking oil. Bake at 350° for 30 to 40 minutes. Serves 4.

● ●

● ● ● ● ● ● ● ● ● ● **Lemon Chicken** ● ● ● ● ● ● ● ● ● ●

1 tsp. thyme leaves

½ tsp. pepper

1 clove garlic, minced

⅓ cup lemon juice, fresh squeezed

4 boneless, skinless chicken breasts

Prepare: Mix all ingredients except chicken breasts together. Pour over chicken breasts in a one-gallon bag.

Freeze: Double bag the chicken. Freeze lying flat.

Serve: Thaw chicken overnight in the refrigerator. Drain marinade. Place chicken breasts in a pan sprayed with light cooking oil. Bake at 350° for 30 to 40 minutes. Serves 4.

● ●

● ● ● ● ● ● ● ● ● ● ● **Pesto Chicken** ● ● ● ● ● ● ● ● ● ●

½ cup prepared pesto

6 boneless, skinless chicken breasts

6 slices mozzarella cheese

Prepare: Pour pesto over chicken breasts in a one-gallon bag.

Freeze: Double bag the chicken. Place the mozzarella cheese in a separate freezer bag and attach to the chicken bag. Freeze lying flat.

Serve: Thaw chicken overnight in the refrigerator. Drain marinade. Place chicken breasts in a pan sprayed with light cooking oil. Place one slice of mozzarella cheese on each chicken breast. Bake at 350° for 30 to 40 minutes. Serves 4.

● ●

• • • • • • • • • • Pizza Roll-Ups • • • • • • • • • • •

1 loaf frozen French, Italian, or all-purpose bread dough

1 lb. lean ground beef or turkey (2½ cups browned)

1 tsp. salt

½ tsp. pepper

2 cups grated part-skim mozzarella cheese

1 tsp. Italian herb seasoning

1 T. chopped fresh parsley

4 cups Italian tomato sauce

Prepare: Thaw dough; roll it into a 14 x 24-inch rectangle about one-quarter inch thick. Brown ground beef or turkey; stir in remaining ingredients except Italian tomato sauce. Spoon filling evenly onto dough, slightly pressing filling into dough. Roll dough lengthwise like a jelly roll and cut into 24 one-inch slices.

Cook: Treat two rimmed cookie sheets with nonstick spray; lay slices on sheets about an inch apart. Preheat oven to 400°. Let roll-ups sit for 10 minutes. Bake for 20 to 25 minutes or until golden brown.

Freeze: Cool roll-ups and freeze in 4 one-gallon bags, 6 per bag. Slip a one-quart bag with 1 cup sauce into each bag of roll-ups.

Serve: Thaw roll-ups and warm them in a preheated 400° oven for 10 minutes or put them frozen in the microwave on high heat for about 2 minutes. Serve with warmed Italian tomato sauce. Serve with tossed green salad. Serves 24.

Note: These roll-ups are super for picnics or nights when the family must eat in shifts. They can be eaten warm or cold. They're also a favorite with kids and an easy snack (and party hors d'oeuvres!)

• •

• • • • • • • • • **Poppy-Seed Chicken** • • • • • • • • • •

4 chicken breasts, cooked and cubed

1 can cream of chicken soup

4 oz. sour cream

2 tsp. poppy seeds, divided

¼ cup melted margarine

½ sleeve Ritz crackers

Prepare: Combine soup, sour cream, and 1 tsp. poppy seeds in a bowl. Crush crackers and combine with melted margarine and remaining poppy seeds. Layer chicken and soup in casserole dish, then top with cracker mixture.

Freeze: Cover and freeze.

Serve: Defrost overnight. Bake at 350° for 30 minutes. Serves 4.

• •

• • • • • • • • • **Sun-Dried Tomato Chicken** • • • • • • • • • •

1 cup sun-dried tomato salad dressing

½ cup sun-dried tomatoes in oil

1 small can sliced black olives

4-6 boneless, skinless chicken breasts

Prepare: Mix all ingredients except chicken breasts together. Pour over chicken breasts in a one-gallon bag.

Freeze: Double bag the chicken. Freeze lying flat.

Serve: Thaw chicken overnight in the refrigerator. Drain marinade. Place chicken breasts in a pan sprayed with light cooking oil. Bake at 350° for 30 to 40 minutes. Serves 4.

• •

• • • • • • • • • Sweet-and-Sour Chicken • • • • • • • • • •

1 cup sugar

2 T. cornstarch

½ cup vinegar

¼ cup soy sauce

¼ tsp. salt

1 clove garlic, minced

½ tsp. paprika

½ tsp. ginger

3 cups chicken breasts, cooked and cubed

1 cup chopped onion

1 cup chopped green pepper

1 cup sliced mushrooms

1 8-oz. can pineapple chunks

Prepare: Drain and keep pineapple juice from can. In a saucepan, combine sugar and cornstarch, whisk together. Then add vinegar, pineapple juice, soy sauce, salt, garlic, paprika, and ginger. Bring to a boil and simmer, stirring until thickened.

Freeze: Pour into freezer bag with chicken, vegetables, and fruit. Freeze.

Serve: Defrost in refrigerator overnight. Reheat in a saucepan and serve over rice. Serves 4.

• • • • • • • • • • • Teriyaki Chicken • • • • • • • • • • • •

(We make this marinade again and again. It's much better than any prepared marinade you can find in the store.)

4 each chicken legs and thighs (or 6 chicken breasts)

½ cup soy sauce

3 T. honey

1 tsp. fresh ginger, grated

2 T. dry sherry (optional)

1 clove garlic, minced

2 green onions, thinly sliced

Prepare: Place the chicken in a gallon plastic bag. Mix the remaining ingredients together in a bowl. Pour the mixture over the chicken and seal the bag.

Freeze: Place bag in another gallon bag and lay flat in the freezer.

Serve: Defrost the chicken. Pour off marinade and bake chicken in a pan at 350° for 30 to 40 minutes or until no longer pink in the center. Serves 4.

• •

Try This at Home

One of the best gifts you can give to yourself is a freezerful of meals. Roger and I set aside a whole day every couple of months as a cooking day. Set aside a Friday and Saturday (Friday for shopping and Saturday for cooking) and tackle four recipes tripled. At the end of the day, you'll have twelve meals ready to nestle into your freezer for some quick dinners on busy nights.

Or as a Group

When my kids were in elementary school, I worked flexible but full-time hours a few years, and I needed to do the whole freezer cooking thing at top speed. I believe it was my friend Vikki who came up with the idea of six of us doing a *freezer swap*. (But I do say with a stupid amount of pride that I came up with the name Six Chicks Freeze and Fix.)

At first we all tried to cook together. It was a lot of work and a lot of fun, but we realized we were giving up one of the greatest benefits of freezer cooking—the ability to cook when it's convenient for you. After our first time, we each cooked at our own homes and then met to swap.

Each of us chose three recipes to cook for our group, and then we each sent the suggested recipes to the rest of the group for discussion.

If, for example, someone suggested a bell-pepper dish, I, being a hater of all things bell pepper, would ask for either a different dish or swap a substitute dish. Here are the three types of meals we would exchange:

- A *marinated meat.* Half the group did chicken breasts, the other half did another meat such as flank steak, pork roast, or pork chops. Then we would swap meats the next month.
- A *casserole.*
- A *wildcard.* These were typically a soup, another marinade, another casserole, or a chili.

Each of us would make six meals for each recipe, so here's a sample of what I would make:

- Six family-sized meals of teriyaki chicken
- Six family-sized meals of baked ziti
- Six family-sized meals of chicken cacciatore

Once I had all my meals prepared, packaged, and frozen, I would pack them all into a couple of coolers and go to the predetermined time and place of the swap, usually at a church or in the Costco parking lot before it opened. Each of us would go home with eighteen different meals. Cool, huh?

Each person paid for the meals they prepared, and we figured it would all even out in the end. However, I love the system Gena Larson from California used with her friends:

> We had a bookkeeper that everyone would call their grocery totals in to, and she would total up the entire amount and split it between the number of participants. Persons who paid more than the average for their groceries would be reimbursed from those whose totals were less than the average. Our average cost per meal usually ranged from $5.50 to $7.00. We were all very money conscious and shopped for meats and other items on sale. If we purchased a spice needed for a recipe, we would write "group" on the

lid and bring it to our next meeting as a pantry item. The cost of those spices were added to grocery totals, so they belonged to all of us. If it was something like salt or garlic, we all used from our own pantries rather than purchase it.

Another great idea is to run a meal-prep ministry through your church. Lynn Kennedy started the Make Ahead Meals ministry at Christ Community Church in Tucson, Arizona. Here is how one of her pupils, and my friend Ruth, describes the ministry:

> Lynn chooses six to eight entrées and sometimes a side (like rice or biscuits). Then she publishes a flyer and offers the class one Thursday each month. Each attendee places an order for what meals they would like to have at the end of the class. Once all the orders are in, Lynn orders the meats through the company our church uses for our kitchen meals, so the cost is reduced.

> She has a team of women who do some of the prep (chopping onions, labeling bags, setting up tables). On the evening of the class, we are divided into groups of two or three depending on how complicated a recipe is or how many batches of a recipe are needed. Then our group will start working on our assignment. For example, I may get assigned the meatball entrée, so I'll work with one other person, and we'll prepare all the ordered entrées for meatballs.

> When everyone is done preparing their assigned recipe, we all shop for what we ordered and paid for before we arrived that night. We are also asked to order and pay for one entrée to donate to our church freezer for use in our Ministry Meals program for families in crisis. It's a lot of work for the organizer, but it's fun for the rest of us, and we go home with however many entrées we ordered. All in all, a great deal.

Chapter 12

Slow Cookers

"Nouvelle cuisine, roughly translated, means:
I can't believe I paid ninety-six dollars and I'm still hungry."

MIKE KALIN

My friend Tina had been pretty adventurous. She decided to do a meat purchase from a grass-fed beef operation, purchasing an assortment of cuts as well as ground beef. Her husband and two boys were excited, and so was Tina—except for one issue. She didn't know what to do with the tougher cuts that were going to arrive on her doorstep.

The ground beef? No problem. She'd turn that into hamburger patties or sauté it up with onions and garlic to put in casseroles. The fillets? Her husband already had his eye on those for grilling.

But in the box of assorted steaks were cuts Tina wasn't familiar with—chuck steaks, skirt steaks, flat-iron steaks...

As we talked about it, I told her that I usually used my slow cooker for those tougher cuts of meat. Pot roast from a cut of chuck in the slow cooker? That is just a little bit of heaven.

What I found strange was Tina's aversion to using the Crock-Pot she'd received as a wedding gift—it had never been out of the box. She had grown up in a home where the only time the Crock-Pot was used was to make stew or some concoction using a condensed soup. She had never considered using it because she had an aversion to cream of mushroom soup.

As I talk with other home cooks, I'm always surprised at the number who don't use a slow cooker. In this day of overscheduled kids, overscheduled parents, tough economic times, and a longing for some comfort food (but wanting to eat healthy at the same time,) my slow cooker is my kitchen's secret weapon.

Here are just a few reasons why I'm so in love with my cooker:

- *No-fuss cooking.* I love that I can throw all the ingredients into the Crock-Pot in the morning and come home in the late afternoon and it's *done.*

- *Stress-free mornings.* I can put the ingredients together the night before, store them in the fridge, and dump them into the Crock-Pot that morning before work.

- *Easy cleanup.* One-pot meals mean one-pot cleanup. I can destroy a kitchen as fast as a rock star can destroy a hotel room. (I'm trying to be better about "clean-as-you-go," but I always leave evidence of where I've been and what I've cooked.)

- *Excellent results.* If I make sure I put enough liquid into the Crock-Pot, I always get a tasty, well-cooked meal.

- *Great for the day of a party.* If we're having a birthday or graduation party (and with four kids, there seems to be one of those every other week), I'll throw together an appetizer or side dish to put in the slow cooker early that morning. That is one dish I don't have to fuss with at the last minute as guests are arriving.

- *Meat tenderizer.* Slow cookers make even the toughest cuts of meat tender when cooked with lots of liquid and not left to sit too long.

Some Slow Cooker Tips

Let the meal equal the pot. The only time I have had poor results with a slow cooker is when I haven't put enough food in the pot. When the pot is too big, food can tend to scorch and dry out. I actually have two slow cookers now—one for meals just for Roger and me (a two-quart), and one for when I know all the kids will be home or I'm making a meal with leftovers to be used in the following night's dinner (a six-quart).

You can overcook. Everyone says, "Just throw it in the pot and forget it!" Well, that's true—to a point. You want to make sure to pay attention to the timing on your meal so it doesn't dry out.

Use a slow cooker with a probe thermometer. If you are always going to arrive home after a meal should be done cooking, you may want to get a slow cooker with a probe thermometer. Our big pot has one of these handy little gadgets and can be programmed to stop cooking when the meat reaches a predetermined temperature.

Make cleanup easier. Use a nonstick cooking spray on the inside of your pot to make cleanup easier.

Brown your meats first. Meats don't brown in the slow cooker, so if you want your meats browned, do it before you put it in the pot.

My Top Five Favorite Things to Cook in the Slow Cooker

● ● ● ● ● ● ● ● ● ● **Slow-Cooker Chili** ● ● ● ● ● ● ● ● ● ●

I love making big batches of chili and serving it with a huge salad and cornbread. The other wonderful thing about doing big batches in the slow cooker is that you can freeze the left-overs for another dinner or in smaller containers for lunch.

2 lb. ground beef round

1 cup chopped onion

2 15-oz. cans red kidney beans, drained

2 14½-oz. cans tomatoes, drained (or six fresh
     tomatoes chopped)

2 cloves garlic, peeled and crushed

2 to 3 tsp. chili powder

1 tsp. black pepper

1 tsp. ground cumin

salt, to taste

In a large skillet, brown ground beef with the chopped onion. Put the ground beef, onions, and other ingredients in a 3½- to 5-quart slow cooker (or if using a 6-quart cooker, just double the recipe). Stir, cover, and cook on low for 9 to 11 hours. Serves 8.

● ●

• • • • • • • • Citrus-Glazed Pork Roast • • • • • • • • •

I love pork roast in the slow cooker for a couple reasons: it doesn't get dried out, and you can cut it to size in order to have just enough to feed your troops.

1 3-lb. boneless pork-loin roast

2 garlic cloves, minced

½ tsp. dried thyme

½ tsp. ground ginger

¼ tsp. pepper

1 T. vegetable oil

1 cup chicken broth

2 T. sugar

2 T. lemon juice

2 T. soy sauce

1½ tsp. orange zest

3 T. cornstarch

½ cup orange juice

Cut roast in half. In a small bowl, combine the garlic, thyme, ginger, and pepper; rub over roast. In a large skillet over medium heat, heat the oil and brown the roast on all sides. Place roast in a 5-quart slow cooker. In a small bowl, combine the broth, sugar, lemon juice, soy sauce, and orange zest; pour over roast. Cover and cook on low for 4 hours or until a meat thermometer reads 160° F. Remove roast and keep warm.

In a saucepan, combine the cornstarch and orange juice until smooth; stir in cooking juices from the slow cooker. Bring to a boil. Cook and stir for 2 minutes or until thickened. Serve with the roast.

• •

Italian Chicken Stew

Rustic—hearty and just plain delicious. Can be served with some warm, grainy bread and a salad.

1 lb. boneless, skinless chicken breasts

1 medium onion, chopped

1 medium zucchini, chopped

4 medium carrots, sliced

4½ cups chicken broth

2 cloves garlic

½ tsp. salt

¼ tsp. pepper

1 cup sliced fresh mushrooms

2 14-oz. cans diced tomatoes, undrained

Shredded Parmesan cheese, if desired

In 3½–4 quart slow cooker, mix onion, zucchini, carrots, broth, tomatoes, mushrooms, garlic, salt, and pepper. Add chicken. Cover and cook on low heat for 5 to 6 hours. Remove chicken and garlic from slow cooker. Mash garlic with a fork. Shred chicken. Return garlic and chicken to slow cooker to keep warm.

To serve, place in soup bowls and top with a slice of French baguette toasted with Parmesan cheese.

Salsa Chicken

Even your surly teenager could throw these ingredients into the pot.

4 boneless, skinless chicken breasts
32 oz. salsa
1 can corn, drained
1 can black beans, drained

Place all ingredients in slow cooker. Cook on low 6 to 8 hours. 30 to 60 minutes prior to serving, remove chicken, shred, and return to slow cooker to keep warm.

Serve over Spanish rice or let everyone prepare their own tortillas using the following ingredients: flour tortilla, sour cream, guacamole, shredded lettuce, diced tomato, shredded cheese, and salsa. Use chicken mixture as filling inside tortillas. Add desired condiments.

Corned Beef and Cabbage

For when you're getting your Irish on—a great, yummy recipe from Julie Carlson:

2 medium onions, sliced
2½ to 3 lb. corned beef brisket
1 cup apple juice
¼ cup packed brown sugar
2 tsp. prepared mustard
6 whole cloves
6 small cabbage wedges

Place onions in slow cooker. Trim fat from brisket. If necessary, cut meat to fit into slow cooker; place on top of onions. In a bowl combine apple juice, sugar, mustard, and cloves; pour over brisket. Place cabbage on top of meat. Cover and cook on low for 10 to 12 hours (or high for 5 to 6 hours). Serves 4.

Chapter 13

When Freezers and Slow Cookers Collide

"I don't like food that's too carefully arranged; it makes me think that the chef is spending too much time arranging and not enough time cooking. If I wanted a picture, I'd buy a painting."

ANDY ROONEY

I love when I find other food nerds out there. It's a title I use—and embrace—lovingly. It's very different from *food snobs* who want to tell you you're using the wrong knife or look down their nose at you if your cheese isn't aged properly. Food snobs can get away with cooking once a week and call themselves a gourmet, but a food nerd is always looking for new ways to make food better and easier. We're the ones who trade recipes at MOPS meetings and steal (with permission) each other's freezer tips for getting dinner on the table.

So let me introduce you to fellow food nerd Kelly Rankin. Kelly and I met at an event where I spoke, and we became friends through my blog. Kelly has taken the concept of freezer meals and slow cooking and done a mash up—freezer/slow cooking.

I am also a freezer/slow cooker, but Kelly's ingenuity for stretching her meals and leaving no leftover left behind is admirable. What follows is her plan for using her freezer and slow cooker for maximum savings of time, energy, and stress.

"I have a version of freezer/slow cooking that has worked really well for me in many meals. Most of my friends and family think I'm crazy, but I know you'll appreciate it. I began using my slow cooker and freezer in tandem for two reasons.

"First, I realized that the portions required for a full, normal-sized slow cooker were wasteful for our family. Our family of five (with small children) will never eat a full roast, and we usually don't eat leftovers. I loved the convenience of a slow cooker, but it made me cringe every time I threw away spoiled leftovers.

"Second, when I figured out that I could use a smaller slow cooker and experience less waste, I realized that I could actually make a normal-sized recipe, but dump half of it in the slow cooker and the other half in a freezer bag for later use. This began my experimentation with freezer/slow cooking.

"My version of freezer/slow cooking varies in complexity. Sometimes it's as simple as dividing a Costco roast into chunked portions that are the perfect size for my family. I then freeze those portions, and when I'm ready to use one, I can easily just throw in a couple carrots, potatoes, other vegetables, and spices. Other times, I do a full recipe and make baggies of slow-cooker meals, with everything ready to be dumped in the slow cooker. Occasionally, it's the other way around; I use my large slow cooker and freeze leftovers for later use. (Yes, I have multiple sizes of slow cookers!)

"One of my biggest discoveries was a mini slow cooker (I use the Proctor Silex 1.5-Quart Slow Cooker). I remember a while back reading that you want a slow cooker to be at least two-thirds full for optimal cooking evenness. I found this out when I tried to make smaller portions in my big slow cooker—things scorched on the edges. This didn't happen with a full slow cooker. This mini slow cooker is the perfect size for my family and allows me to fill it up without using a ton of food. It won't work once my kids get older and start eating more, but for now it helps me stretch my food budget."

I love it—no food is wasted, she can prepare in advance, and you know anything made in a slow cooker is going to be good.

Slow Cooker to Freezer

Some of my favorite slow-cooker-to-freezer recipes are soups, stews, and chili. You can double or triple (in a 6-quart slow cooker) a soup recipe, and after it cools, bag it up in gallon bags to be reheated another time.

Here are a couple of other recipes to make in the slow cooker and store in the freezer for a busy night of running kids around:

● ● ● ● ● **Slow Cooker Smoked Pulled Pork BBQ** ● ● ● ● ●
(Kelly Rankin)

"Four simple ingredients and a day of slow cooking lead to an amazingly simple, economical, and delicious pork BBQ. No smoker is needed, and the leftovers freeze beautifully for a later meal. The liquid smoke and beef bouillon are the essential keys to this simple recipe, giving the pork a great flavor with minimal BBQ sauce. Perfect for a large gathering."

Prep time: 10 minutes

Cook time: 7 to 9 hours

Yields: 10 servings

5-lb. pork sirloin tip roast

2 T. liquid smoke (typically found with condiments)

2 T. beef bouillon (*not* broth)

⅓ cup water

Serve with your favorite BBQ sauce, to taste

Place pork roast in a large slow cooker. Pour water, liquid smoke, and bouillon on top of pork roast. Cook on high for 7 to 9 hours, flipping roast once during cooking, if possible, to allow the juices to simmer all sides of the meat. Meat is finished cooking when it easily pulls apart with a fork. Remove roast from slow cooker and pull pork apart. Return pork to slow cooker and add BBQ sauce to taste, or serve BBQ sauce on the side. Great on sandwiches or by itself.

To freeze: Place cooked BBQ in 1-quart freezer bags, removing air. Thaw, rewarm, and serve. Keeps in freezer up to 6 months.

● ●

Freezer to Slow Cooker

● ● ● ● ● ● ● ● ● **Roast Beef Sandwiches** ● ● ● ● ● ● ● ● ●
(Kelly Rankin)

"Cook the meat in your slow cooker and have a sandwich ready in ten minutes. Great with a side of creamy horseradish."

Prep time: 10 minutes

Cook time: 12 hours

Ready in: 12 hours, 10 minutes

Yields: 16 servings

1 4-lb. boneless beef roast

½ cup soy sauce

1 tsp. beef bouillon

1 bay leaf

1 tsp. dried rosemary

1 tsp. dried thyme

1 tsp. garlic powder

8 red peppers, sliced

16 slices Swiss cheese

16 French rolls

mayonnaise or creamy horseradish

In a medium bowl, combine soy sauce, bouillon, bay leaf, rosemary, thyme, and garlic powder. Pour mixture over roast and add enough water to almost cover roast. Cover and cook on low heat for 10 to 12 hours, or until meat is very tender. Add peppers in the last hour of cooking.

Remove meat from broth, reserving broth. Slice meat very thin (I prefer an electric knife) and distribute on rolls for sandwiches. Cover meat with Swiss cheese and broil on high for approximately 5 minutes, or until cheese is melted. Serve with mayonnaise or creamy horseradish.

● ●

"This roast-beef-sandwich recipe is another one that I subdivide into smaller portions prior to cooking, freeze these dinner-sized portions, then cook in my small slow cooker. I package the meat and sauce together, and in a separate bag, I also package a few slices of Swiss cheese along with the rolls. The meat simmers all day, and the sandwiches take only a few minutes to put together."—Kelly

• • • • • • • • • • **Beef Pepper Stir-Fry** • • • • • • • • • •
(Kelly Rankin)

"I have divided this into smaller portions to stick in the freezer uncooked. On the day I want to serve it, I thaw it and cook it in my mini slow cooker, serving over rice."

2 lb. beef sirloin, cut into 2-inch strips

garlic powder to taste

3 T. vegetable oil

1 cube beef bouillon

¼ cup hot water

1 T. cornstarch

½ cup onions, chopped

2 large green bell peppers, roughly chopped

1 14.5-oz. can stewed tomatoes, with liquid

3 T. soy sauce

1 tsp. sugar

1 tsp. salt

Sprinkle strips of sirloin with garlic powder to taste. In a large skillet over medium heat, heat the vegetable oil and brown the seasoned beef strips. Transfer to a slow cooker. Mix bouillon cube with hot water until dissolved, then mix in cornstarch until dissolved. Pour into the slow cooker with meat. Stir in onion, green peppers, stewed tomatoes, soy sauce, sugar, and salt. Cover and cook on high for 3 to 4 hours, or on low for 6 to 8 hours.

● ● **Slow Cooker Herbed Pork with Stuffing and Apples** ● ●
(Kelly Rankin)

A slow cooker favorite! A great combination of herbs, spices, and sweetness.

Prep time: 20 minutes

Cook time: 4 hours

Yields: 6 servings

2½ tsp. sugar

¾ tsp. dried marjoram

¾ tsp. rubbed sage

½ tsp. salt

¼ tsp. celery seed

¼ tsp. ground mustard

⅛ tsp. pepper

2 lb. boneless pork loin roast

4 Granny Smith apples

¼ cup water

1½ cups cranberries

1 package Stove Top Stuffing mix

Combine the first seven ingredients; rub over roast. Cover and refrigerate for 4 hours or overnight (preferred, not required).

Place herb-rubbed pork in slow cooker, surrounded by cranberries and apples. Gently pour water around pork. Cook on high for 4 hours or low for 6 to 8 hours. In the last 10 minutes prior to serving, dump the stuffing mix on top of roast, mixing it in the juices. Allow it to cook for a few more minutes, until the stuffing is softened.

Chapter 14

LeftOvers On Purpose (LOOP) Meals

*"Leftovers in their less visible form are called memories.
Stored in the refrigerator of the mind and the cupboard of the heart."*

THOMAS FULLER

My friend Gerry and I were having a deep meaningful talk about Thanksgivings past. No, we weren't reflecting on all the things we were grateful for, we were remembering our food traditions. (My mouth starts watering just thinking about turkey gravy.)

She told me that one year she was just tired of putting on the whole show, so she decided they would eat in a restaurant. The food was yummy, and they had a great time relaxing and letting someone else cook and clean up. It wasn't until the next day that Gerry saw the fatal flaw in her plan: No leftovers. How were they going to construct on Friday those turkey-and-cranberry sandwiches with dressing and gravy that were almost as much a tradition as anything that happened on Thursday?

An ode to the leftover!

One of my main strategies for saving time and money when it comes to meal planning is LeftOvers On Purpose (LOOP) meals. It's a pretty simple idea. If I'm making a pork roast on Sunday for my family, I make a little extra (LeftOvers On Purpose) for pork carnitas for Tuesday night's dinner. I usually look at it this way: Once a week I'm making a big, meat-centric meal, such as a roasted chicken or a pot roast. If I don't plan for what happens with the leftovers, there's a fifty-fifty chance they will either:

1. Be eaten by a ravenous twenty-year-old boy in our house
in less time than it takes to toast a piece of bread, or

2. Get shoved to the back of the fridge, not to be seen again
   until the next "what is growing on that back shelf?" cleanup.

So planning ahead to use those leftovers on purpose saves me time, money, and almost a night of cooking.

Why I Love LOOP Meals

They save time. It takes just as much effort to cook two pounds of chicken as it does four. So what if it takes a little longer in the oven? I don't have to fuss with it.

They save money. Every time I make a meal from leftovers, I feel like a financial genius. In my mind, it's like eating for free.

They lessen the guilt. I no longer feel remorse when I hear my grandmother's voice in my head saying, "Waste not, want not."

They are not just leftovers. They are leftovers cleverly disguised as a delicious new meal. Even those picky men who say they won't eat leftovers will never know the difference. (And if your husband fusses at the notion, just explain that restaurants do this all the time. Yesterday's unsold roasted chicken becomes today's chicken noodle soup.)

They make me smarter. I never feel more like a kitchen ninja than when I'm being smart about my meal planning. LOOP meals are the ultimate in planning.

To make a LOOP meal happen, you may want to have your first half of the meal (the pork roast, the big ham, the roasted chicken) over the weekend when you have a little more time, and then the second half on a weeknight where the main ingredient is already sitting there in your fridge, waiting to be turned into LOOP magic.

One final hint—before you serve your family that first meal of yummy pot roast or roasted chicken, set aside what you'll need for the second meal. If the chicken is as delicious as usual, you may not be able to count on leftovers.

My Favorite LOOP Meals

In the rest of this chapter I provide recipes for my favorite LOOP meals made from either pork, beef, or chicken. I devote a section to each of these meats and begin with a base recipe followed by additional recipes for using the leftovers from the main meat dish. In other words, start with a fab dinner, and then create more fab dinners—without the extra cooking. Genius, right?

LOOP Pork Roast Recipes

● ● ● ● ● ●**Lemon, Garlic, and Thyme Pork Roast**● ● ● ● ● ●
(Kathi Lipp)

¾ tsp. lemon zest

½ tsp. salt

2 thyme sprigs

¼ tsp. pepper

3 garlic cloves, minced

1 cup chicken broth

2 lb. pork loin roast

In a medium-sized bowl, combine the first six ingredients. Place pork roast in a large container and marinate for at least 3 hours or overnight. Place pork in an 11 x 7-inch casserole and pour the broth, minus the thyme leaves, over the roast. Position a meat thermometer in the center of the pork roast. Bake at 400° for 30 minutes. Turn pork over, and bake an additional 35 minutes or until thermometer registers 160°. Discard broth. Serves 8 (or reserve one-third to one-half the roast for another recipe).

Round It Out With: Roasted potatoes with salt-and-olive-oil rub and carrot salad.

● ●

Some LOOP recipes you can make with the leftover pork:

● ● ● ● ● ● ● ● ● ● ● ● ● **Pork Stir-Fry** ● ● ● ● ● ● ● ● ● ● ● ●
(Kathi Lipp)

leftover pork cut into approximately ½-inch by 2-inch slices

3 T. extra-virgin olive oil

1 medium carrot, sliced

2 green bell peppers

1 medium yellow onion, chopped

salt and freshly ground black pepper

4 T. soy sauce

1 T. cornstarch

1 T. light brown sugar

2 tsp. garlic, minced

1 T. white wine vinegar

Halve, stem, seed, and de-vein the bell peppers; dice small. Put the soy sauce, cornstarch, sugar, garlic, and vinegar in a medium-sized mixing bowl and stir until the cornstarch has dissolved completely. Add the pork slices and toss until the pork is thoroughly coated. Set aside.

Heat the olive oil in a wok or large skillet on high. Stir-fry the pork until lightly browned, about 3 minutes. Add the bell pepper, onion, and carrot, season to taste with salt and pepper, and cook about 3 to 5 minutes more.

Round It Out With: Brown rice.

● ●

Golden Rice and Pork
(Kathi Lipp)

2 T. cooking oil

1 cup uncooked rice

2½ cups onion, sliced

½ tsp. salt

2 chicken bouillon cubes

2½ cups boiling water

2 tsp. soy sauce

2 stalks celery, sliced

2 cups leftover pork, cut in strips

Heat oil in large frying pan. Add rice, onions, and salt. Cook over medium heat until golden, stirring constantly. Remove from heat for 5 minutes. Dissolve bouillon cubes in boiling water and pour over rice mixture. Cover and cook about 30 minutes until rice is tender. Stir in celery, and pork. Cover and cook another 5 minutes. Stir in soy sauce and serve.

Pulled Pork Sandwiches
(Kathi Lipp)

leftover pork

1 bottle favorite BBQ sauce

1 package buns, such as kaiser rolls, hamburger buns, or Sweet Hawaiian rolls

Shred leftover pork roast with a fork or two. Place in the slow cooker with the BBQ sauce and cook on low for 3 to 5 hours. Serve on buns.

● ● ● ● ● ● ● ● ● ● **Carnitas Recipe** ● ● ● ● ● ● ● ● ● ● ●
(Kathi Lipp)

2 lb. leftover pork roast, cubed

1 quart beef broth

1 cup chunky tomato salsa (prepared or homemade)

water

8-12 corn tortillas

2 cups fresh tomato salsa (pico de gallo)

In a large skillet, combine pork, beef broth and chunky tomato salsa. Add enough water to cover the pork. Cover and bring to a boil, then reduce and let simmer for 3-4 hours until the pork is tender. Preheat oven to 400°. Remove meat from liquid in pot (discard the liquid) and spread the meat over a roasting pan. Break the meat into small chunks. Roast meat for 15 to 20 minutes until brown and crispy.

Follow the package instruction for warming the tortillas. Place the carnitas on top of the tortilla. Top with salsa. Serves 6 to 8.

Round It Out With: Grated lettuce (lightly salted and sprinkled with vinegar), beans, avocados, and grated cheese.

LOOP Pot Roast Recipes

We have really cut back on our consumption of red meat—for health reasons as well as the cost. So when I decide to make a pot roast, we are going to enjoy every last morsel.

● ● ● ● ● ● ● ● ● **Old-Fashioned Pot Roast** ● ● ● ● ● ● ● ● ● ●
(Kathi Lipp)

1 rump or pot roast

2 bouillon cubes dissolved in 2 cups hot water

1 tsp. garlic, chopped

1 envelope onion soup mix

Mix the dissolved bouillon, garlic, and onion soup mix together. Place roast in the slow cooker and pour the mixture over the roast. Cook on low for 8 to 10 hours or until tender.

• •

Some LOOP recipes you can make with the leftover beef:

• • • • • • • • • • • **Beef Stroganoff** • • • • • • • • • • • •
(Kathi Lipp)

1 lb. leftover pot roast

5 oz. egg noodles, uncooked

4 tsp. vegetable oil

1 clove garlic, minced

½ lb. mushrooms, sliced

1 package (1¾ oz.) brown-gravy mix

1 cup cold water

¼ cup sour cream

salt and pepper to taste

Cook noodles according to package directions. Keep warm. Cut roast into 1-inch wide strips. In large nonstick skillet, heat 2 tsp. oil over medium heat until hot. Add beef and garlic and stir-fry for about 3 minutes. Remove from skillet and add salt and pepper.

In the same skillet, cook mushrooms in remaining 2 tsp. oil for 2 minutes or until tender. Add gravy mix and water; blend well and stir until thickened. Return beef to skillet, heat for 1 minute, and serve over noodles. Add a spoonful of sour cream on top.

• •

Beef Taquitos
(Kathi Lipp)

3 cups (approximate) leftover pot roast
2 T. taco sauce
salt and pepper to taste
Tabasco sauce to taste
1 package small corn tortillas
1 cup cooking oil

Shred pot roast and add seasonings. Heat oil to high. Place one tortilla at a time in oil, flipping the tortilla quickly to get it soft, then remove from pan. Add meat mixture and roll tortilla into a tube. Place in frying pan again until crisp and lightly browned.

Round It Out With: Guacamole

Roger's Guacamole
(Roger Lipp)

2 avocados
1 T. lemon juice
4 cloves fresh garlic, crushed
1 bunch green onions, white parts finely chopped
½ tsp. black pepper
¼ tsp. salt
1 tsp. oregano
1 tsp. basil
1 tsp. jalapeño chopped (can substitute Anaheim for
    milder guacamole)

Remove skins and pits of avocados and mash. Add lemon juice, garlic, and green onion and mix in. Add in seasonings and jalapeño.

Round It Out With: Salsa and sour cream

● ● ● ● ● ● ● ● ● ● **BBQ Beef Sandwiches** ● ● ● ● ● ● ● ● ● ●
(Kathi Lipp)

leftover pot roast

1 bottle favorite BBQ sauce

1 package buns, such as kaiser rolls, hamburger buns,
   or Sweet Hawaiian rolls

Shred roast using a fork or two. Place in the slow cooker with BBQ sauce and cook on low for 3 to 5 hours. Serve on buns.

● ●

● ● ● ● ● ● ● ● ● ● ● **Easy Cottage Pie** ● ● ● ● ● ● ● ● ● ●
(Kathi Lipp)

1 lb. leftover pot roast, shredded

1 T. vegetable oil

2 carrots, whole and peeled

½ small onion, chopped

1 tomato, chopped

2 T. Worcestershire sauce

¼ tsp. salt

6 potatoes, boiled and mashed (or 1 small
   package instant potatoes)

Preheat oven to 350°. In a large skillet, warm the oil over medium heat. Using a potato peeler, shave carrots letting the shavings fall into the pan. Add tomatoes and onion and continue to sauté over medium heat. Add the shredded pot roast, Worcestershire sauce, and salt. Stir for another minute and remove from heat.

Pour the beef mixture into casserole dish. Top with mashed potatoes and score with a fork. Bake for 35 minutes or until potatoes are just brown and crisp at the edges.

● ●

· · · · · · · · · · · · **Beef and Orzo** · · · · · · · · · · · · ·
(Kathi Lipp)

1 lb. leftover pot roast, shredded

1 14½-oz. can stewed tomatoes, undrained

½ cup celery stalk, sliced

½ cup orzo, uncooked

½ tsp. salt

2 garlic cloves, pressed

Put all ingredients in a 10-inch skillet sprayed with nonstick spray. Heat to boiling, then reduce heat. Cover and simmer about 12 minutes, stirring frequently, until liquid is absorbed and pasta is tender.

· ·

LOOP Roasted Chicken Recipes

I don't know what I would do without the all-purpose chicken. On Mondays and Thursdays, I often throw a few frozen chicken breasts into the oven in a shallow pan covered with aluminum foil and bake them at 350° for about 45 minutes. Those become the basis of a lot of lunches for me—shredded chicken in my salad, chicken pizzas, chicken in pitas.

But I feel like even more of a kitchen ninja when I roast a chicken and have leftovers to turn into other meals. And let's be honest—if I've done a big Costco run, my reward is picking up one or two of their yummy roasted chickens and: (1) having that for dinner with a big salad and rosemary bread, and (2) taking the meat off the second chicken and using it for casseroles or other LOOP chicken recipes. (It's OK to cheat on home cooking when the chickens from Costco are sooooo good.)

Roast Chicken
(Kathi Lipp)

1 whole chicken (approximately 4 lb.)

1 head garlic, peeled and chopped

8 sprigs fresh rosemary

2 lemons, whole

2 T. extra-virgin olive oil

1 tsp. salt

½ tsp. fresh-ground black pepper

Preheat oven to 475°. Thoroughly rinse the chicken inside and out, and pat dry with paper towels. Remove rosemary from 4 of the stems and chop coarsely; reserve the rest for later. Slice lemons into quarters. Put garlic, lemons, and the chopped rosemary into the chicken's cavity. Rub the chicken skin generously with the olive oil and season with salt and pepper. Place the chicken on a rack in a roasting pan and put remaining rosemary stems on the chicken, around wings and drumsticks. (If you don't have a rack and roasting pan, a small cooling rack set in a 9 x 13 dish works well, or put the chicken straight into a casserole. Just make sure to oil the pan first.)

Roast chicken in the preheated oven for 15 minutes. Decrease oven temperature to 375° and cook approximately 60 to 75 minutes more. It's done when you insert a meat thermometer into the thickest part of the thigh, but not near bone or fat, and it registers 180° to 185° (time depends a lot on weight).

Allow chicken to rest at least 15 minutes before carving.

Some LOOP recipes you can make
with the leftover chicken:

• • • • • • Chicken Salsa Avocado Pita Pocket • • • • • •
(Kathi Lipp)

1 lb. leftover chicken, sliced

1 small jar of salsa, drained

1 avocado, sliced

4 whole-wheat pita pockets

Warm the pita pockets in oven or toaster oven until soft and pliable. Cut the top one-third off the pita pocket and gently open the pocket. Mix the chicken and drained salsa together. Fill the pita pocket with one-fourth of the chicken-salsa mixture and avocado. Serves 4.

• • • • • • • • • • • Chicken Curry • • • • • • • • • • • •
(Kathi Lipp)

1 lb. leftover chicken, shredded

1 T. extra-virgin olive oil

¼ cup raisins (optional)

1 medium onion, sliced

salt and freshly ground pepper to taste

1½ tsp. yellow curry powder

1 cup sour cream

cilantro or parsley, chopped

Put the oil in a large skillet over medium-high heat. When hot, add the onions and raisins (if desired). Sprinkle with salt and pepper and cook, stirring occasionally, until translucent, about 5 minutes. Turn the heat down to medium, add leftover chicken and stir into onions. Sprinkle with the curry powder and continue to cook a minute or two. Add the sour cream and stir constantly over medium-low heat until the mixture is nice and thick. Garnish with cilantro or parsley and serve with rice. Serves 4.

• •

• • • • • • • • • **Chicken and Pasta Salad** • • • • • • • • • •
(Kathi Lipp)

1½ cups leftover chicken, chopped

2 cups shell pasta (cooked, rinsed, and cooled)

½ red pepper

½ green pepper

8-10 cherry tomatoes, halved

¼ cup feta cheese, crumbled (optional)

¼ cup Caesar salad dressing (more or less to taste
     and to coat)

Chop peppers and add to tomatoes in large bowl. Add chicken, pasta, and feta. Add Caesar salad dressing and mix well. Refrigerate until needed.

• •

This gives you an idea of how to create LOOP meals—cooking once and eating twice with half the effort and twice the yum.

Chapter 15

Pantry Meals

"To eat is a necessity, but to eat intelligently is an art."
FRANÇOIS DE LA ROCHEFOUCAULD

Sometimes, your plans don't go according to plan.

The meat that you planned to take out this morning to defrost is still tucked away in the back of your freezer. Or the soccer game went into overtime and there's no time to run by the store.

That's when your pantry's supplies will stand up off the shelves and save the day.

Look over the following recipes and figure out which ones could save the day the next time you didn't make it to the store, or your daughter just called to say she's bringing over a friend (or six).

● ● ● ● ● ● ● ● ● ● ● ● ● **Kathi's Chili** ● ● ● ● ● ● ● ● ● ● ● ● ●

A less-spicy version that even kids will like. Most of the ingredients are straight from the pantry. Plus, if you already have some cooked ground beef with onions and garlic stashed in the freezer (one of the staples of our deep freeze), the meal practically makes itself.

¾ lb. ground turkey or beef

1 cup chopped onions

1 clove garlic, minced

1 16-oz. can stewed tomatoes

1 16-oz. can kidney beans, drained

1 16-oz. can tomato sauce

3 tsp. chili powder

½ tsp. basil

1 6-oz. can tomato paste

In a large saucepan, cook ground turkey, onions, and garlic until the onions are translucent and the meat is brown. Drain. Stir in undrained tomatoes, drained kidney beans, tomato sauce, chili powder, basil and tomato paste. Bring to a boil. Reduce heat and simmer, covered, for 30 minutes. Serves 4.

● ●

A Purely Pantry Pasta Dish
(Cheryl Knowles-deMartine)

"My favorite pantry meal is a super quick-and-easy (and good!) pasta dish. Served with a salad, you have a meal."—Cheryl

1 small onion, chopped

2 cloves garlic, chopped

1 T. olive oil

1-2 cans chopped tomatoes

1 can chopped black olives, drained

1-2 jars chopped marinated artichokes

4 cups pasta of your choice, cooked

Parmesan cheese

Sauté onion and garlic in olive oil. Add tomatoes, black olives, and artichokes. Toss this mixture with pasta and sprinkle a bit of Parmesan cheese on top. If you want a little extra protein, add 1 drained can of cannellini or black beans to the tomato mixture.

● ●

Black Bean Corn Salsa
(Autumn Hicks)

1 can black beans, drained and rinsed

1 can corn, drained and rinsed

¼ cup green onions, chopped

1 tsp. cilantro, chopped

1 tsp. jalapeño chopped

2 T. lime juice (or to taste)

Stir ingredients together and chill or just eat. Yummy!

Black Bean Soup
(Esther Cowan)

2 cans black beans, rinsed and drained

1 can chicken broth

1 can cream of chicken soup

1 can Mexican corn

1 16-oz.jar salsa (choose hotness you like)

Optional toppings: Mexican cheese, sour cream,
    crumbled tortilla chips.

Mix together and cook several hours in a slower cooker without the lid on. Garnish with Mexican cheese and a dollop of sour cream or crumbled tortilla chips. Serve with cornbread or chips.

● ● ● ● ● ● ● ● ● ● **Wild Rice Casserole** ● ● ● ● ● ● ● ● ● ●
(Cheri Gregory)

1 4-oz. box wild rice

1 onion, chopped

1 16-oz. can stewed tomatoes

1 2¼-oz. can sliced olives

1 4-oz. can sliced mushrooms with juice

1 8-oz. can tomato sauce

½ lb. cheddar cheese, shredded (approximately 2½ cups)

¼ pound Swiss cheese, shredded (approximately 1 cup)

Rinse wild rice thoroughly several times. Sauté chopped onion in a small amount of butter or margarine. Combine all ingredients and pour into a covered casserole dish. Bake at 250° for 3 hours. Remove cover for the last 15 minutes of baking.

● ●

● ● ● ● ● ● ● ● ● ● ● **Chicken Tortilla Soup** ● ● ● ● ● ● ● ● ● ●
(Kathi Lipp)

1 can tomato soup

1 large can chicken broth

4 cups water

1 package taco seasoning

4 boneless, skinless chicken breasts

1 can corn

Optional toppings: Jack or cheddar cheese, tortilla chips, green onions

Cook and shred chicken breasts. Mix together tomato soup, chicken broth, water, taco seasoning, chicken, and corn. Place in a saucepan and simmer for 20 minutes. Serves 4.

We serve this with corn quesadillas and vegetarian refried beans.

● ●

Pantry S'mores Brownies
(Regena Florenti)

(I know it's not a dinner recipe, but who couldn't use a good emergency dessert when your son brings over a half-dozen friends all looking as if they might eat the paint off your kitchen baseboards.)

18 whole graham crackers

1 stick butter, melted

1 box dark chocolate fudge brownie mix

½ bag mini-marshmallows

1 cup semisweet chocolate chips

Preheat oven to 350°. Spray a 9 x 13 pan and line with parchment paper; include the sides of the pan.

To make the crust: Crush or food process graham crackers. When finely crushed, add melted butter and mix. Press firmly into pan, reserving a few tablespoons for the topping.

To make the brownie layer: Prepare brownie batter according to package directions. Spread brownie batter carefully over crust and bake according to package directions. Take out of oven and turn oven to broil, keeping the wire rack on the middle to lower level. Sprinkle marshmallows over hot brownies. Add the chocolate chips and reserved graham cracker mixture. Broil until marshmallows are golden brown. (This goes *very* fast. *Do not* take your eyes off it.)

Cool completely. Slices best with a lightly oiled pizza cutter.

Chapter 16

Fast Food at Home

*"I went into a McDonald's yesterday and said, 'I'd like some fries.'
The girl at the counter said, 'Would you like some fries with that?'"*

JAY LENO

Fast food has a very bad reputation.

It's bad for you, it has too many calories, too much fat, and is a terrible rut to fall into. That is, fast food that you order through a drive-through intercom.

Fast food at home is a whole different thing. Fast food at home is a staple in most homes and a much better alternative (cheaper, healthier, and better tasting) than resorting to figuring out what number to order at McJack-n-Bell.

Here are some of our family favorites that are faster than drive-through and a whole lot tastier.

• • • • • • • • • **Instant Pepperoni Calzones** • • • • • • • •
(Kathi Lipp)

1 can premade pizza crust

20 turkey pepperoni slices

⅓ cup marinara sauce

1 cup Colby/cheddar cheese mix, shredded

Preheat oven to 400°. Roll out pizza dough on a floured cutting board. Cut the dough into quarters and shape each quarter into a square. Put five pepperoni slices on one half corner of each square.

Mix together the cheese and marinara sauce. Place a spoonful on top of the pepperoni. Repeat on each of the dough squares. Fold each square in half, corner to corner; seal edges with fork. Put on baking sheet sprayed with cooking spray.

Bake for 20 to 22 minutes or until golden brown. Serves 4.

Williams's Enchilada Casserole
(Monica Williams)

1 large can green enchilada sauce

1 large can chicken breast

8-10 tostadas

2 cups shredded mozzarella or Jack cheese

⅓ cup Parmesan cheese

Optional:

½ cup chopped onion

1 small can sliced olives

In a sprayed baking dish, layer one-half the enchilada sauce, all the chicken, one-half the tostadas, one-half the shredded cheese, one-half the onion, and olives. Finish with a layer of tostadas, sauce, shredded cheese, and top with Parmesan. Bake covered at 350° until bubbling; uncover and bake 5 minutes or until cheese looks golden brown. Serve with a dollop of sour cream and chopped onion and a side of refried beans and salad.

All-Purpose Veggie Mix
(Linda Jenkins)

"Here's a replication of the vegetable mix that was in a vegetarian sandwich I fell in love with at a restaurant. I like to sauté these vegetables, and you can use the mix in many different recipes, such as the ones that follow."—Linda

2 T. extra-virgin olive oil

1 green bell pepper, chopped

1 red bell pepper, chopped

1 medium red onion; quarter, slice, and break apart

2 cloves garlic

1 can quartered artichoke hearts in water;
    slice quarters in half

½ can black olives, sliced

8 mushrooms, sliced

Pour olive oil in a skillet and turn heat to medium high (you can use a little more oil if needed). When pan is hot, drop in the green and red bell peppers along with the onions. Grate or finely chop the garlic cloves over the pan. When the vegetables are as tender as you like them, add the artichoke hearts, olives, and mushrooms. Heat through until the mushrooms are slightly cooked.

• •

Use this vegetable mix in the following recipes:

• • • • • • • • • • • **Sandwiches** • • • • • • • • • • • •

2 T. prepared pesto

⅓ cup mayonnaise

4 hoagie rolls

All-Purpose Veggie Mix, pp. 174-75

4 slices of provolone cheese (or grated mozzarella,
    if you prefer)

Mix the pesto and mayonnaise together. Slice the rolls open and toast lightly under broiler. Spread the pesto mayonnaise evenly over the top and bottom halves of rolls. Place spoonfuls of veggie mix on the bottom half of each roll. Place one slice of provolone cheese over veggies. Place under broiler again to melt cheese.

• •

● ● ● ● ● ● ● ● ● ● ● ● **Appetizers** ● ● ● ● ● ● ● ● ● ● ● ● ●

2 T. prepared pesto

⅓ cup mayonnaise

1 fresh-baked baguette

All-Purpose Veggie Mix, pp. 174-75

5-6 slices of provolone cheese (or grated mozzarella,
    if you prefer)

Mix the pesto and mayonnaise together. Slice baguette into
1-inch slices and toast lightly under broiler. Spread pesto mayonnaise evenly over each slice. Place spoonfuls of veggie mix
on the slices. Place ¼ slice of provolone cheese over veggies.
Place under broiler again to melt cheese.

● ●

● ● ● ● ● ● ● ● ● ● ● ● **Calzone** ● ● ● ● ● ● ● ● ● ● ● ● ●

fresh pizza dough

1 jar prepared pesto

All-Purpose Veggie Mix, pp. 174-75

1 cup mozzarella cheese, grated

1 cup provolone cheese, grated (or sliced, if you prefer)

Preheat oven to 400°. Follow directions on pizza dough to create crust, or roll out dough to create the size circle you want.
You can make individual calzones or one big enough for the
family. Lightly spread pesto over center of dough. Spoon veggie mix in the center of circle. Place cheese over top. Fold
dough over and, using either water or some egg whites, wet
the edges together and pinch to close. Place 2 to 3 slits in top
of dough to allow steam to escape. Place on a cookie sheet
and in the preheated oven. For large calzone, cook for around
25 minutes (check at 15); for individuals, check at 12 minutes.

● ●

Vegetarian Pizza

2 T. prepared pesto

1 jar Alfredo sauce

All-Purpose Veggie Mix, pp. 174-75

precooked pizza crust

1 cup mozzarella cheese, grated

1 cup provolone cheese, grated (or use sliced, if you prefer)

⅓ cup Parmesan cheese, grated

Preheat oven to 400°. In a bowl, mix the Alfredo sauce and pesto together. Place the pizza crust on a round baking pan. Spread sauce evenly over crust. Spoon veggie mix over top. Place slices of provolone cheese on pizza until covered with a single layer. Sprinkle over top the mozzarella and Parmesan cheeses. Bake until hot and bubbly, around 12 minutes.

• • • • • • • • • Asian Chicken Wrap Ups • • • • • • • • • •

While this may not be the fastest meal in the west (prep time 20 minutes), it's "no cook" if you buy the chicken precooked. And everyone can construct their own wrap, saving you time!

2 cups skinless chicken breast, cooked and chopped
   (or chop up strips from precooked chicken breasts)

3 T. rice vinegar

1½ T. light soy sauce

1½ tsp. sesame oil

¼ cup green onions, chopped

¼ cup almonds, sliced

seasoned salt and pepper

¼ cup crispy rice noodles

1 cup carrots, shredded

1 cup broccoli, shredded

4-6 butter lettuce leaves

⅓ cup peanut sauce

⅓ cup Asian salad dressing for dipping sauce

In a medium glass bowl, combine chicken, vinegar, soy sauce, sesame oil, green onions, and almonds. Mix well. Season to taste with seasoned salt and pepper. Cover and refrigerate for an hour.

On platter, arrange lettuce leaves and small containers of peanut sauce and Asian dressing. Place a mound of the chicken mixture on each lettuce leaf. Top with crispy noodles, carrots, and broccoli. Roll up the leaf and dip in one of the sauces. Serves 4 as appetizers or 2 as a main course.

• • • • • • • • **Chicken and Bean Tostada** • • • • • • • • •

1 ripe avocado, peeled

1 cup plus 2 T. tomato, finely chopped and divided

3 T. fresh onion, minced and divided

3 T. fresh lime juice, divided

½ tsp. salt, divided

1 small garlic clove, minced

1 T. fresh cilantro, chopped

1 T. seeded jalapeño pepper, minced

2 cups boneless, skinless chicken breast,
    cooked and shredded

¼ tsp. smoked paprika

8 6-inch corn tostada shells

1 cup salsa

First, prepare the guacamole: Place avocado in a small bowl and mash with a fork. Stir in 2 T. tomato, 1 T. onion, 1 T. lime juice, ¼ tsp. salt, and garlic, and then 1 cup tomato, 2 T. onion, 1 T. lime juice, ¼ tsp. salt, cilantro, and jalapeño; mix well.

Combine chicken, remaining 1 T. juice, and paprika; mix well. Spread about 1 T. guacamole over each tostada shell, and top each with ¼ cup chicken mixture and about 2 T. salsa. Serves 4 (serving size: 2 tostadas).

• • • • • • • • Creamy Dill Turkey Roll-ups • • • • • • • • • •

6 green onions, chopped

6 T. fresh chives, chopped (or 4 T. dried)

½ T. onion powder

1 12-oz. container whipped low-fat cream cheese

¾ cup Greek yogurt

8 whole-wheat tortillas

4 oz. turkey, thinly sliced

2 cups lettuce, shredded

2 medium tomatoes, chopped

The night before, in a food processor, blend well the green onions, chives, onion powder, cream cheese, and Greek yogurt. Refrigerate overnight.

Spread the cream-cheese mixture on the tortillas. Spread the turkey, lettuce, and tomatoes evenly over the cream cheese. Roll each tortilla into a wrap.

• • • • • • • • Pesto Chicken Croissants • • • • • • • • •

¼ cup pesto

¼ cup reduced-fat mayonnaise

1 package precooked chicken strips

4 butter croissants

Combine pesto and mayonnaise in a small bowl. Cut chicken stripes into 1-inch chunks. Mix chicken and mayonnaise. Cut croissants length-wise and fill with chicken mixture. Serves 4.

Jambalaya
(Amy Spergers)

1 onion, finely chopped

2 cloves garlic

2 T. butter or oil

1 cup cooked ham, diced

1 cup chicken, cooked and cut up

½ lb. ground Italian sausage, browned

1 green bell pepper, chopped (optional)

2 stalks celery, chopped (optional)

2 T. parsley flakes

1 tsp. salt

¼ tsp. thyme

¼ tsp. pepper (all seasonings are to taste)

¼ tsp. cayenne pepper

1 bay leaf

2 15-oz. cans diced tomatoes

3 cups chicken broth

1 cup long-grain rice (white or brown)

1 lb. cooked shrimp

In large pot, sauté onion and garlic in butter or oil; add cooked meats except shrimp. If adding bell pepper and celery, do so now. Cook until onion and veggies are tender. Add to pot the chicken broth, tomatoes, parsley, salt, thyme, pepper, cayenne pepper, and bay leaf. Cover and bring to a boil.

Remove cover; keeping a continuous boil, stir in rice. Cover and cook 20 to 30 minutes more until rice is cooked through. Add the cooked shrimp and heat through. (Do not cook longer or the shrimp will become tough.)

Serve *hot*!

Chapter 17

Eat Your Veggies

"Vegetables are a must on a diet.
I suggest carrot cake, zucchini bread, and pumpkin pie."

JIM DAVIS

For the longest time, vegetables were an afterthought in my house. I admit it. I was so stressed out getting dinner on the table that if I threw on a bagged salad or a handful of carrots, I considered myself lucky. (My kids, however, would prefer that I forgot altogether.)

But now that I have more than a few yummy (and healthy) veggie recipes in my kitchen arsenal, veggies often become the star of the dinner instead of playing a supporting role.

Here are just a few of my favorites to get you inspired.

Artichokes

If you aren't familiar with how to clean and prepare an artichoke, here are the basic steps as outlined by the California Artichoke Advisory Board:

1. Wash artichokes under cold running water.

2. Pull off lower petals that are small or discolored.

3. Cut stems close to base. (Use stainless knives to prevent discoloration.)

4. Cut off top quarter and tips of petals, if desired. (Some people like the look of clipped petals, but it isn't necessary to remove the thorns. They soften with cooking and pose no threat to diners.)

5. Plunge into acidified water to preserve color. (One tablespoon vinegar or lemon juice per quart of water.)

6. *Optional*: The trimmed artichoke stems are edible. Cut brown end about one-half inch. Peel fibrous outer layer to reach tender green of stem. Stem may be steamed whole with the artichoke. Cut into rounds or julienne for salads or pastas.

When Roger and I joined a farmers' co-op, we would get bundles and bushels of all sorts of weird-looking veggies. Finally, the highly recognizable artichokes arrived. Hurray! Just a few weeks before receiving ours, we had been served grilled artichokes in a bistro in Chico, California. Roger found this recipe and tweaked it a bit to get the flavors just right.

● ● ● ● ● ● ● ● ● ● **Grilled Artichokes** ● ● ● ● ● ● ● ● ● ●

4 large artichokes

¾ cup olive oil

2 T. McCormick Vegetable Supreme Seasoning

4 cloves garlic, chopped

1 tsp. salt

½ tsp. ground black pepper

Cut tips off the artichokes and then cut in half length-wise. Bring a large pot of water to a boil. Meanwhile, preheat an outdoor grill for medium-high heat.

Add artichokes to boiling water, and cook for about 15 minutes. Drain. Squeeze out the extra water in the artichoke. In a small bowl stir together the olive oil, Vegetable Supreme, and garlic. Season with salt and pepper.

Brush the artichokes with a coating of the oil-garlic mix and place them on the preheated grill. Grill the artichokes for 5 to 10 minutes, basting with dip and turning frequently, until the tips are a little charred.

● ●

• • • • • • • • • • • **Stuffed Artichokes** • • • • • • • • • • • •

4 large artichokes

2 tsp. lemon juice

2 cups Italian breadcrumbs, toasted

½ cup grated Parmigiano-Reggiano cheese (or Parmesan)

½ cup fresh parsley, minced

2 garlic cloves, minced

2 tsp. Italian seasoning

1 tsp. lemon peel, grated

½ tsp. pepper

¼ tsp. salt

1 T. olive oil

Level the bottom of each artichoke and cut 1 inch from the tops. Using kitchen scissors, snip off tips of outer leaves. Stand artichokes in a Dutch oven; add 1 inch of water mixed with lemon juice. Bring to a boil. Reduce heat; cover and simmer for 30 to 35 minutes or until leaves near the center pull out easily.

In a colander, turn the artichokes over so that their leaves point down; let stand for 10 minutes. With a spoon, carefully scrape out the fuzzy center portions of artichokes and discard.

In a small bowl, combine the breadcrumbs, cheese, parsley, garlic, Italian seasoning, lemon peel, pepper, and salt. Add olive oil; mix well. Gently spread artichoke leaves apart; fill with breadcrumb mixture.

Place in an 11- x 7-inch baking dish coated with cooking spray. Bake uncovered at 350° for 15 to 20 minutes or until filling is lightly browned. Serves 4.

• •

Asparagus

● ● ● ● ● ● ● ● ● ● **Asparagus Parmesan** ● ● ● ● ● ● ● ● ● ●

This has to be the world's easiest asparagus recipe. We eat it a few times a week when asparagus is in season and when Roger isn't BBQing.

12 medium fresh asparagus spears, trimmed

2 T. extra-virgin olive oil

2 T. Parmesan cheese, grated

¼ tsp. garlic salt

Brush asparagus spears with oil and place on a baking sheet coated with nonstick cooking spray. Bake uncovered at 400° for 6 minutes; turn asparagus. Bake 6 minutes longer or until asparagus is tender.

Combine Parmesan cheese and garlic salt; sprinkle over asparagus as soon as it comes out of the oven. Serve immediately.

● ●

● ● ● ● ● ● ● **Asparagus with a Side of Onions** ● ● ● ● ● ● ● ●

My friend Barb threw this together one night when I stopped over for dinner. She was too embarrassed to give me the recipe, but after a lot of begging (and some subtle threats) she revealed her secret ingredient—onion soup mix.

2 lb. fresh asparagus, trimmed

¼ cup butter

1 T. dry onion soup mix

½ cup mozzarella cheese, shredded

Place asparagus in a steamer basket. Place in a large saucepan or skillet over 1 inch of water; bring to a boil. Cover and steam for 4 to 5 minutes or until crisp-tender. In a small saucepan, melt butter.

Add soup mix to the melted butter. Cook and stir for 1 minute or until heated through.

Remove asparagus to a serving dish. Drizzle with butter and onion mixture; sprinkle with mozzarella cheese and serve.

● ●

● ● ● ● ● **Tiger Tails Bacon-Wrapped Asparagus** ● ● ● ● ●

When Roger proposed to me on a cookout at Big Basin State Park he made me Stuffed Portobello Mushrooms and these Tiger Tails. If he weren't already such a great guy I might have said yes just because anything wrapped in bacon makes me woozy.

1 lb. fresh asparagus

8 to 10 strips bacon

In the oven: Preheat oven to 400°. Wash and trim asparagus spears. Cut bacon strips in half crosswise. Wrap one-half strip bacon around each asparagus spear, leaving tip and end exposed. Lay spears on a baking sheet with sides and bake for 20 to 25 minutes, or until bacon is cooked. Serve warm or at room temperature.

On the grill: Follow above directions, but use wooden skewers to keep the bacon in place. Grill on BBQ until the bacon is cooked. Serve immediately. Makes 16 to 20 spears.

(If you want to be even more decadent, you can serve this with a lemon-mayo dip.)

● ●

Broccoli

● ● ● ● ● ● ● ● **Orange Broccoli and Carrots** ● ● ● ● ● ● ● ●
(Kathi Lipp)

⅓ cup orange juice

1 T. dry sherry

1 tsp. cornstarch

1 T. extra-virgin olive oil

1 tsp. gingerroot, grated

1½ cups carrots, thinly bias-sliced

1 cup broccoli florets

For sauce: In a bowl, stir together orange juice, dry sherry, and cornstarch and set aside. Preheat a wok or large skillet over high heat. Add oil. Stir-fry gingerroot in hot oil for 15 seconds. Add carrots and stir-fry for 1 minute. Add broccoli and stir-fry for 3 to 4 minutes or until crisp-tender. Push vegetables from the center of wok or skillet. Stir sauce and add to center of wok; cook and stir until thickened and bubbly. Stir in vegetables; serve immediately. Serves 4.

● ●

● ● ● ● ● ● ● ● ● ● ● **Broccoli Salad** ● ● ● ● ● ● ● ● ● ● ●

Salad:

2 bunches broccoli, florets only (5 to 6 cups florets)

1 medium red onion, chopped

½ cup raisins

10 to 12 slices bacon, fried and crumbled

Dressing:

1 cup low-fat mayonnaise

2 T. balsamic vinegar

2 tsp. sugar

Separate florets from broccoli stalks. (Stems can be used in another casserole or in soups.) Combine salad ingredients; top with dressing mixture. Chill and serve.

● ●

• • • • • Broccoli with Garlic Butter and Cashews • • • • •

1½ lb. fresh broccoli, chopped

⅓ cup butter

1 T. brown sugar

3 T. soy sauce

2 tsp. white vinegar

¼ tsp. black pepper, ground

2 cloves garlic, minced

⅓ cup salted cashews, chopped

Place broccoli into a large pot with about 1 inch of water in the bottom. Bring to a boil and cook for 7 minutes, or until tender but still crisp. Drain.

Melt butter in a small skillet over medium heat. Mix in brown sugar, soy sauce, vinegar, pepper, and garlic. Bring to a boil, remove from heat. Mix in cashews, and pour the sauce over the broccoli. Serve immediately.

• •

Carrots

• • • • • • • • • • Minted Carrots • • • • • • • • • •

2 cups carrots, sliced

½ cup water

2 T. butter

2 T. sugar

2 T. fresh mint, chopped

Steam carrots over boiling water about ten minutes, or until tender. In a saucepan, melt butter and add sugar and carrots, stirring until sugar melts. Immediately before serving, add mint and toss lightly. Serve hot. Serves 4.

• •

● ● ● ● ● ● ● ● ● ● ● **Baked Carrots** ● ● ● ● ● ● ● ● ● ● ●

4 cups carrots, sliced

½ cup water

2 T. sugar

1 tsp. nutmeg

1 tsp. salt

6 T. butter

In a casserole dish, mix the sugar, nutmeg, and salt with water. Add the carrots and place slices of butter on top. Bake at 350° for 10 minutes, stirring after 5 minutes.

● ●

Corn

An ear of sweet corn is made up of several parts. The main parts are the shank, husk, silk, cob, and kernels.

● ● ● ● ● **Roger's Corn, a Deconstructed Recipe** ● ● ● ● ●

Select ears that are still completely in husks. When selecting your corn, you can peel the top of the husk back just a tiny bit to make sure the corn is good.

Throw ears, husks and all, on the grill over a medium-high heat. No prep is needed. Turn frequently. Grill for 10 to 15 minutes. The outer husk layers will burn, but don't worry. The corn inside is fine (actually, it's delicious)!

To eat, peel back the husk carefully. The closer you get to the corn, the hotter the husks will be. Have a garbage bag ready to receive the husks. Be sure to get all the silk strings off the corn too.

This is so good there's no need for butter or salt. Just eat!

● ●

• • • • • **Summer Smokey Ham and Corn Salad** • • • • •

⅓ cup reduced-fat sour cream

2 T. distilled white vinegar

1 tsp. smoked paprika

¼ tsp. salt

1 large bag prewashed salad (mixed baby greens are best)

1 medium tomato, diced

¼ cup green onions, diced

1 cup canned corn, drained

1 cup croutons

¾ cup cooked ham, diced (about 4 oz.)

Prepare the dressing by mixing the sour cream with the vinegar, paprika, and salt. Pour the dressing over the salad and toss. Top with the rest of the ingredients.

• •

Mushrooms

• • • • • • • • **Pan-Roasted Mushrooms** • • • • • • • • •

3 T. extra-virgin olive oil

8 cups mushrooms, sliced

3 T. water

¼ cup butter

2 cloves garlic, minced

1 T. fresh chives, chopped

salt and pepper to taste

Heat olive oil in a large pan. Add mushrooms and water. Cook without stirring for about 8 to 10 minutes or until mushrooms are golden. Remove from heat and add rest of ingredients. Season to taste.

• •

Tomatoes

Yes, I'm well aware that tomatoes are technically a fruit. But when was the last time you wanted to mix some heirloom tomatoes in with your strawberries and peaches for a nice fruit salad?

Capresi Salad

4 large red or yellow tomatoes, sliced

1 lb. mozzarella cheese, drained and sliced

1 bunch fresh basil leaves

¼ cup extra-virgin olive oil

¼ cup red balsamic vinegar

salt and freshly ground black pepper

Arrange tomato slices, cheese slices, and basil alternately overlapping on platter. Whisk together oil and vinegar. Pour over tomatoes, cheese, and basil. Season to taste with salt and pepper.

Tomato Cucumber Feta Salad Recipe

1 T. lemon juice

2 tsp. olive oil

coarse salt and freshly ground black pepper to taste

2-3 cups cherry tomatoes, sliced

1 cup cucumber, peeled and chopped

¼ cup feta cheese, crumbled

2 T. green onions, finely chopped

1 T. fresh oregano, finely chopped

Prepare dressing by combining lemon juice, olive oil, salt, and pepper. Toss dressing with tomatoes, cucumber, feta, onions, and oregano. Serves 4.

Zucchini

● ● ● ● ● ● ● ● ● ● ● **Stir-Fry Zucchini** ● ● ● ● ● ● ● ● ● ●

4 cups zucchini, sliced

¼ cup extra-virgin olive oil

1-2 tsp. oregano to taste

2 tsp. sugar

1 tsp. salt

Sauté the zucchini in skillet with olive oil and seasonings until tender, about 15 minutes, stirring frequently. Serves 6.

● ●

● ● ● ● ● ● ● ● **Zucchini and Mushrooms** ● ● ● ● ● ● ● ●

4 medium zucchini, grated

1 tsp. salt

½ lb. mushrooms, sliced

¼ cup butter

¼ cup green onions, sliced

1 clove garlic, minced

½ cup sour cream

1 T. fresh basil, chopped

Combine the zucchini and salt and let stand. Heat the mushrooms in a skillet, shaking over high heat until the liquid evaporates. Add butter to skillet. Once butter is melted, add green onion and garlic to the pan and keep stirring. Squeeze excess liquid out of zucchini. Add to onions, garlic, and mushrooms and stir occasionally over heat for 5 minutes. Stir in the sour cream and basil, heat and serve. Serves 3 to 4.

● ●

Making Dinnertime Matter

"The dinner table is the center for the teaching and practicing not just of table manners but of conversation, consideration, tolerance, family feeling, and just about all the other accomplishments of polite society except the minuet."

JUDITH MARTIN

You've pulled it all together—you have planned for, shopped for, and cooked a great meal. Now it's time to set the table for a dinner with conversation and connection.

Table Talk—40 Dinnertime Conversation Starters

Pick one topic a night to discuss at the dinner table.

1. Do you prefer dogs or cats? Why?

2. If you were given three wishes, what would they be?

3. If you were the president, what problem would you work on first?

4. If you were going to a deserted island and could take only three items, what would they be?

5. If you could ask God one question, what would it be?

6. If you could be invisible for a day, what would you do?

7. If you could spend a whole day with any person in the world, who would it be?

8. *Adult*: Name five things in the house that you did not have

growing up. *Child*: Which of those things would you miss the most?

9. If you could take a weeklong vacation anywhere in the world, where would you go?

10. If you had a time machine, where would you go and why?

11. So far, what has been the happiest day of your life?

12. What is your most valued possession?

13. Who was your favorite teacher? Why did you like him or her?

14. What is your favorite room in your house? Why?

15. What is your favorite way to spend time with your friends?

16. If you could make one chore disappear, which one would it be?

17. What is your favorite thing to do that is absolutely free?

18. What is your favorite game? How did you learn to play it?

19. What is your favorite fast-food place? What do you like to order there?

20. What is one of your favorite smells?

21. What is one job you've always wanted to try, even if it were just for a day?

22. What is one family tradition you enjoy?

23. What is something that always makes you laugh? A joke, a movie, a friend?

24. What is your favorite time of year—winter, spring, summer, or fall? Why?

25. What is your favorite day of the week? Why?

26. What is your favorite candy?

27. What is the best thing you ever did for your birthday?

28. Would you rather go to a play or go on a hike? Why?

29. What was the first thing you ever learned to cook on your own?

30. What is the best novel you've ever read? What is the best nonfiction book? Why do you love them so much?

31. What is your favorite song? What memory do you associate with that song?

32. What is your ideal way of spending a Sunday afternoon?

33. If you could eat only one food for the rest of your life, what would it be?

34. Growing up, what was your favorite toy?

35. What is your favorite piece of clothing? Why do you like it? (It's comfortable, I like how it looks, etc.)

36. What is the best gift you've ever been given? Why did you like it so much?

37. What one new skill would you like to learn in the next year?

38. What is one thing that happened this week that you are thankful for?

39. What is your favorite thing to write with? A pen, a pencil, chalk, crayons, or something else?

40. What is your favorite animal? Do you think it would make a good pet?

INDEX OF RECIPES

Dear Reader,

Thanks for being a part of The "What's for Dinner?" Solution. One of the greatest privileges I have is to hear back from the people who have used my books. I would love to stay in touch.

On the web: www.KathiLipp.com
E-mail: Kathi@ProjectsForYourSoul.com
Facebook: facebook.com/kathilipp.author
Twitter: twitter.com/kathilipp
Mail: Kathi Lipp
      171 Branham Lane
      Suite 10-122
      San Jose, CA 95136

- Opportunities for input and discussion with other readers are available at www.ProjectsForYourSoul.com.

- If you are leading a group through The "What's for Dinner?" Solution, check out the "For Leaders" section at www.ProjectsForYourSoul.com.

In His Grace,
Kathi Lipp

About the Author

Kathi Lipp is a busy conference and retreat speaker and an author who inspires women to take beneficial action steps in their personal, marital, and spiritual lives. She has written *The Husband Project: 21 Days to Loving Your Man—on Purpose and with a Plan; The Marriage Project: 21 Days to More Love and Laughter;* and *The Me Project: 21 Days to Living the Life You've Always Wanted.* In addition, her articles have appeared in *MomSense Magazine, MOPS Connection Leaders Magazine, Bay Area Parent,* and *Focus on the Family.* She is also a food writer for Nickelodeon TV's *Parents Connect.*

Church leaders and women's ministry directors rely on Kathi to help women move from living out of obligation to enjoying godly passion. She shares her cheerful humor and biblical insights across the U.S. at conferences and retreats.

Kathi and her husband, Roger, are the parents of four young adults and live in San Jose, California.

The Husband Project

21 Days of Loving Your Man— on Purpose and with a Plan

Keeping a marriage healthy is all about the details—the daily actions and interactions in which husbands and wives lift each other up and offer support, encouragement, and love. In *The Husband Project* women will discover fun and creative ways to bring back that lovin' feeling and remind their husbands—and themselves—why they married in the first place.

Using the sense of humor that draws thousands of women a year to hear her speak, Kathi Lipp shows wives through simple daily action plans how they can bring the fun back into their relationship even amidst their busy schedules.

The Husband Project is an indispensable resource for the wife who desires to

- discover the unique plan God has for her marriage and her role as a wife
- create a plan to love her husband "on purpose"
- support and encourage other wives who want to make their marriage a priority
- experience release from the guilt of "not being enough"

The Husband Project is for every woman who desires to bring more joy into her marriage but needs just a little help setting a plan into action.

The Marriage Project

21 Days to More Love and Laughter

More love, more laughter—more lingerie.

What would marriages look like if for 21 days, husbands and wives put their marriage on *project status*? Plenty of books describe how to improve marriage, how to save a marriage, and how to ramp up the intimacy in a marriage. In *The Marriage Project*, Kathi Lipp shows readers how to put the *fun* back in marriage with 21 simple yet effective projects, such as doing something they enjoyed together before they got married or flirting with their spouse via e-mail or text messages.

Each of the projects contains:

- a project description
- suggestions for how to complete the project
- reports from other couples on how they accomplished the project
- a prayer
- a place to record project results

In addition to the daily projects, three bonus projects encourage couples to turn up the heat in the bedroom.

For couples who haven't given up on the dream of being head-over-heels with their spouse again, *The Marriage Project* provides just the right boost.

Included are tips on how to use *The Marriage Project* to revitalize marriages in a local church or small group.

The Me Project

21 Days to Living the Life You've Always Wanted

Most women in the midst of careers, marriage, raising children, and caring for parents set their personal goals aside. *The Me Project* provides women with fun and creative ways to bring back the sense of purpose and vitality that comes with living out the plans and dreams God has planted in their hearts. Kathi Lipp's warm tone and laugh-out-loud humor will motivate women to take daily steps toward bringing purpose back into their lives and give them the confidence they can do it in spite of busy schedules.

A woman who reads and applies *The Me Project* will

- discover the unique plan God has for her life and her role as a wife, mother, worker, or volunteer
- gather a community of like-minded women who want to make their goals a priority
- change her attitudes toward her roles in life, as well as how she approaches her personal goals

This handy guide coaches women to do one simple thing toward achieving their goals each day for three weeks, bringing a sense of vitality and exhilaration back into their lives.